TAKING A
STAND *for*
GOD

Dear Lawrence,

May these messages of
God through this faithful
servant touch your heart.

Love,
John & Dm——
1988.

TAKING A STAND FOR GOD

First Chinese Baptist Church
Los Angeles, California

TAKING A STAND FOR GOD

Scripture quotations are from the New American Standard Bible,
© 1960, 1962, 1963, 1968, 1971, 1972, 1973, 1975, 1977 by The Lockman
Foundation. Used by permission.

ISBN 0-945304-00-5
Library of Congress Catalog Card Number
Printed in the United States of America

PREFACE

Gregory R. Owyang, known to our young people as Dr. Greg, came to our church in 1970, as a young seminary student aspiring to be a pastor. Some commented then, "He's so young! How could he serve in a church such as ours?" Later, while preaching at a youth conference in the East coast, he came early and sat unnoticed among the young people. Much to everyone's surprise as he came forward when being introduced, people were astonished that such a young preacher could minister to such a large congregation. Yet, our great God makes no mistakes. He knew, called and appointed His servant even before he was born (Je. 1:5).

Greg preached his very first sermon at the First Chinese Baptist Church on Good Friday, 1971. He was enthusiastic, but his lack of experience was evident. Undaunted, he took every opportunity to preach and to serve the Lord in every way. I personally was impressed and inspired by his unquenchable spirit for learning and contagious enthusiasm for doing. Even after his seminary days, he took numerous opportunities to call our Senior Pastor, Dr. Timothy Lin, to ask questions about the Bible and about preaching.

As a fellow seminary student and later as a fellow pastor at FCBC, I saw God's hand upon this young preacher. In travelling to places throughout the United States and Canada where Greg had preached, I found that many testified as to how his messages had brought them to Christ, revived their spiritual lives and changed them in marvelous ways.

With the sudden home going of Greg in 1985, many of the friends, brothers and sisters who have grown to know this young, dynamic and gifted preacher remarked, "What a loss for the people of the succeeding generations, who would not have the same opportunity." This book is therefore a compilation of some of the messages Greg has preached at the First Chinese Baptist Church. These messages are collected, so that those who did not have the opportunity to be under his public ministry may also be challenged and blessed. Greg's messages were characterized by his boldness in declaring the truth of God, as rooted in the rich soil of Scripture, and illuminated by his colorful illustrations and concrete suggestions for application. The sermons contained within this volume are thereby profitable for application and meditation.

In short, Greg's preaching is a rich blend of Scriptural integrity and practical insight, through which it is hoped this book would be a testimony of God's goodness. His messages and life are lovingly dedicated "to the only God our Saviour, through Jesus Christ our Lord, be glory, majesty, dominion and authority, before all time and now and forever. Amen" (Jude 25).

Murphy Lum
Assistant Pastor

Los Angeles, California
October 20, 1987

ii

FOREWORD

I want to lead our congregation to enter into the presence of God. I want to lead you there, so you will be able to enjoy and relish the presence of God. Come to His presence and stay awhile, that your faith will grow.
— "Lord, Increase Our Faith!"

Every worship service together with Dr. Greg was indeed sweet, joyous and peaceful. Through him, understanding towards our God, towards Satan and towards the purpose and manner of Christian living has reached a higher caliber. Having been bestowed with such a great blessing, our church thinks that it is only proper for us to transcribe and publish Dr. Greg's sermons in book form, and share God's revelation to him with brothers and sisters of this age, that Christians of all local churches may stand firm for God and not lose sight of God's Kingdom.

The church has over two hundred cassette tapes of Sunday sermons delivered by Dr. Greg. More than seventy of them have been transcribed. Among these that were transcribed, sixteen sermons representing different aspects of his theology were chosen to collaborate this volume.

Each transcription has been carefully checked and re-checked at least three times with a variable speed cassette player. Editing was done only when absolutely necessary to achieve clarity, so as to preserve the sermons in their original form. Headings and subheadings were added to each sermon primarily based on outlines submitted by Dr. Greg and later printed on our Sunday bulletins. All quotations of the Bible are according to the New American Standard Bible version. This volume exists in both English and Chinese.

With solemn reverence, the church offers to God the Father, God the Son and God the Holy Spirit our humble thanks for His helping hand in bringing this publication to completion. The church also expresses deep appreciation to the large team of brothers and sisters who have devoted their time and love to this work. May our great God be glorified and Christians be edified through it.

Praise the Lord! Amen.

The Editorial Committee
First Chinese Baptist Church

List of Abbreviations

Gn. - Genesis

Ex. - Exodus

Lv. -Leviticus

Nu. - Numbers

Dt. - Deuteronomy

Jos. - Joshua

Jdg. - Judges

Ru. - Ruth

1 Sa. - 1 Samuel

2 Sa. - 2 Samuel

1 Ki. - 1 Kings

2 Ki. - 2 Kings

1 Ch. - 1 Chronicles

2 Ch. - 2 Chronicles

Ezr. - Ezra

Ne. - Nehemiah

Est. - Esther

Jb. - Job

Ps. - Psalms

Pr. - Proverbs

Ec. - Ecclesiastes

Ct. - Song of Solomon

Is. - Isaiah

Je. - Jeremiah

La. - Lamentations

Ezk. - Ezekiel

Dn. - Daniel

Ho. - Hosea

Joel - Joel

Am. - Amos

Ob. - Obadiah

Jon. - Jonah

Mi. - Micah

Na. - Nahum

Hab. - Habakkuk

Zp. - Zephaniah

Hg. - Haggai

Zc. - Zechariah

Mal. - Malachi

Mt. - Matthew

Mk. - Mark

Lk. - Luke

Jn. - John

Acts - Acts

Rom. - Romans

1 Cor. - 1 Corinthians

2 Cor. - 2 Corinthians

Gal. - Galatians

Eph. - Ephesians

Phil. - Philippians

Col. - Colossians

1 Thes. - 1 Thessalonians

2 Thes. - 2 Thessalonians

1 Tim. - 1 Timothy

2 Tim. - 2 Timothy

Tit. - Titus

Phm. - Philemon

Heb. - Hebrews

Jas. - James

1 Pet. - 1 Peter

2 Pet. - 2 Peter

1 Jn. - 1 John

2 Jn. - 2 John

3 Jn. - 3 John

Jude - Jude

Rev. - Revelation

CONTENTS

	Preface	i
	Foreword	iii
	List of Abbreviations	v
I	Taking A Stand For God	1
II	Take Hold Of Eternal Life	17
III	How Personal Is Your God?	31
IV	He Who Is Spiritual - Part I	43
V	He Who Is Spiritual - Part II	55
VI	When I Cry, God Is Silent	67
VII	God's Grace To Do God's Will	77
VIII	Spiritual Warfare	93
IX	What Happens When I Sin?	107
X	The Battle Within	123
XI	Lord, Increase Our Faith!	137
XII	How To Love God	151
XIII	To Be Great In God's Kingdom	167
XIV	Let Us Not Lose Sight Of Our Purpose	181
XV	Wanted: Sons Of Encouragement	193
XVI	A Missions-Minded Church	207
	Appendix:	
	In Remembrance of	
	Gregory Robert Owyang	223
	Chronology of the Sermons	227

TAKING A STAND FOR GOD

If at a wedding banquet somebody at your table makes this comment, "Nobody believes in God anymore," what will you do? Maybe, at a funeral, you are told by relatives to face the casket and bow three times to the deceased. What will you do as a Christian? If somebody comes knocking on your door selling magazines and you discover that he is a Jehovah's Witness selling the Watchtower magazine, what will you do?

You and I are constantly faced with situations that test our Christian convictions. We admire men and women of the Bible, because they stood upon their convictions even at the cost of their lives. We also notice that when they took a stand for God, they not only glorified God but also brought significant changes to their generation. This is sorely missed among us. We need people who can stand for God and who can make an effective change in our generation.

A Great Example

You say, "How can I do anything? I'm so insignificant." Ah, you underestimate yourself, and you underestimate your God. I would like us to see some of the principles in the Bible. There are many men and women in the Bible we can look at. Today, I want us to look at Elijah. We are so impressed with the prophet Elijah. We know of his great victory and his great despair. When we think of Elijah, we think of his departure from this earth and his appearance at the transfiguration on the mount with Jesus Christ. Elijah, what a terrific Bible character he is.

An unbelieving world Will you turn with me to 1 Kings 17:1:

> Now Elijah the Tishbite, who was of the settlers of Gilead, said to Ahab, "As the LORD, the God of Israel lives, before whom I stand, surely there shall be neither dew nor rain these years, except by my word."

The background of this passage begins with the nation of Israel having suffered many things. There was civil war and the nation was divided into two: the Kingdom of the North and the Kingdom of the South. Our focus here is on the Kingdom of the North—Israel. An evil king had come to the throne. King Ahab was known not only for his evil deeds but also for his marriage to an evil woman, the Queen Jezebel. Jezebel was the one who brought in the worship of the false god Baal. It was a terrible worship in which believers sacrificed children. Archaeologists have dug up the bones of many of these children that had been sacrificed to Baal. At that time, Israel was convinced that Baal was god and that the true God, Yahweh, must be dead. All of Israel followed Baal, and the prophets of Baal through Jezebel killed all the prophets of the Lord. Then entered Elijah the Tishbite in chapter seventeen.

2

A humble heritage   The Tishbites were settlers of Gilead. We know where Gilead was, but we do not know much about the Tishbites. That is not important. It does not matter where you are from. Maybe you are from Hong Kong; maybe you are from somewhere in China; maybe you are from America; maybe you are from Alhambra. People in the world would say, "What's Alhambra?" It does not matter where you are from. It does not matter what your family background is. You can be an ordinary person. We do not know where Elijah came from. The Bible just mentions his name right here in verse one.

A God-fearing name   Elijah is a wonderful name with a significant meaning. The "El" stands for "God," and "jah" stands for "Yahweh, the Lord." His name means "the Lord is God." When all of Israel was thinking that the Lord was dead and that Baal must be the true God, Elijah bore the name, "the Lord is God." You also bear a significant name. You bear the name of Christian. You bear the name of Jesus Christ. You bear the name of the one true God who came in the flesh, and you are to bear this name of significance to this generation. In order for others to know that God has come to this world, we have to take a stand for our God. If we are going to stand for God, we better meet the requirements.

A convincing proclamation   Elijah said:

"As the LORD, the God of Israel lives...." (1 Ki. 17:1)

A few years ago here in America, the headline—"God is dead"—hit the newspaper. There are many who feel the same today. People cannot sense the vitality of God. Look at all the people going after different cults: the many thousands in Jehovah's Witnesses; those following the Mormon religion; and those involved in spiritism, going after mediums, witches, séances and checking horoscopes. People go after different religions to look for supernatural things. Where did the cults get these people from? They got them from the Baptists, the Presbyterians and the Methodists. These people in the cults came out from Christian churches, because when they went to the Christian Church, they could not find God. And it seems they turned to other religions and cults thinking that God was there. They came out from Christian churches, because Christians in the Church today are not standing for God.

"As the LORD, the God of Israel lives," said Elijah. What will convince the world that God is alive? The one thing that will convince people is seeing the vitality of God in our lives. God is not alive because of huge, beautiful cathedrals, or because of great numbers of people. After all, at that time there was only one Elijah, while there were 850 false prophets. Such a number still did not prove that Baal was a true god. All it takes is one man or one woman who is dynamically enthusiastic about the vitality of God and who is convicted that God changes lives and changes people.

The Requisites

Know your God When a person says that he knows God, there ought to be some evidence. What evidence is there in your life? You say that you know God. In your life what has happened that you cannot explain except by supernatural means? Have you changed any attitudes? Have you overcome any bad habits? Your temper has been changed. Is it because something supernatural happened, which you have no way of explaining except that "God did something to my life"? Is there anything like that in your life? Or, is everything in your life merely natural? You are just the product of your environment. You are the way you are, because that is the way you were raised. Is there anything in your life you cannot

4

explain except that it must be from God? I know there are many such things in my life.

Do you know that God is living? This world is groping in the dark, searching for light and seeking for positive proof that God is alive. People are not going to see it unless they see it in you. My children are not impressed that I am a pastor of this church. What they see is how I am at home. How are you wherever you are? Is God really living? Is the reality and the consistency of God's vitality in your heart?

Represent your God Elijah said, "before whom I stand. . . ." Elijah was convinced and he had the audacity to believe that he was a personal representative of the living God. "I stand before God! He is the one I serve!" What boldness he had! Brothers and sisters, you too, are the representatives of God. So many of you do not know that. You are either going to be a good representative or a bad one. If you begin to know this and if you are convinced that you are His representative, that will revolutionize your life. You stand before others, because you stand before God. You are a personal representative of the living God. You do not represent any other authority; but all authorities are given to you to be His representative. If you are involved in sin or worldly pursuits, you are a bad representative. If you know whom you are representing, you would count it such a privilege and honor— "the Almighty God, and I am His representative!" You need to be convinced that you are a representative of the living God and be conscientious of this fact.

The Lord revealed this to me many years ago. I used to worry about possessing the label or title of being a pastor, because when people know that you are a pastor, you are going to be good. "Of course you are that way because you are a pastor." You see, people always have these stereotypes of a pastor. How can I really be a good witness for the Lord?

5

Maybe, it is better if I am not a pastor but a lay Christian. Then, people will be amazed and I may have a better testimony. But God said to me, "Don't worry about what your title is. You are my representative no matter what your title is."

I remember years ago I was preaching in New York. When I go to a conference, I like to sit in the back to watch how people sing and how they react in the meeting. This was a young people's conference. Finally, they introduced the speaker, Dr. Owyang. Everybody looked around. "Where is he?" I got up from the back, I walked forward and people were shocked. They thought that I would be an elderly Chinese fellow with grey hair, black rimmed glasses, black suit and white shirt—the stereotype of a pastor. But, I was so young. Then I spoke to them, and again they were shocked: no Chinese accent! My English is so good. They thought that it was really nice, and they began to relax. A couple of girls at the back began talking and making a lot of disturbances. I stopped my preaching and said, "You two girls over there stand up. Don't talk when I talk. Sit down." They were shocked again: so strict, so conservative. Ah! They did not know what to make of me. I am so young, I speak such good English, I am so strict and I am a pastor! Then, I brought up my guitar and started playing my guitar. They were so confused because I was not the stereotype.

Do you know that you are God's personal representative? Do not be stereotyped. Elijah did not care that he was a prophet of God. Jezebel killed all the prophets, but Elijah still took a stand for God. You have to know that you are God's personal representative, and be His personal representative no matter how young, how old or who you are.

Obey your God The Word of the Lord came to Elijah in verse two, telling him to go eastward; and in verse four, the Lord said:

> you shall drink of the brook, and I have commanded the
> ravens to provide for you there.

"Elijah, just go over there to the east. The birds are going to bring you bread." "Sure, God!" That would be our response. "You want me to go out to the wilderness, and you're going to send birds to bring food to me. Who has ever heard of such a thing?" But what does the Bible say?

> So he went and did according to the word of the LORD....
> (v. 5)

Elijah knew how to obey God. It did not happen overnight. He had to learn God's Word and learn to obey it. He had to develop and cultivate a lifestyle of obedience. You and I need to learn to do that too. There are small things that God tells us to do. If we just do them accordingly, we will begin to develop a lifestyle of obedience. One day, God may tell us to do something very unusual and we may say, "Ah, God, that's impossible." Yet because we have developed a lifestyle of obedience, we will do it automatically. What will happen then? God will do exactly as He says. The birds came and fed Elijah. When we learn the lifestyle of obedience, we will watch miracles happen in our lives.

Years ago, God told me, "You be a preacher." My first reaction was "No, that's impossible." But God taught me obedience. My family members did not like it. I had to take a stand for God and learn to obey Him. God started working miracles in my life. For me, to stand here before you today is a miracle. God has worked a lot of miracles in my life. You need to obey the Lord. Obey! Obey! Learn to obey! One day, God may tell you something very unusual. Maybe He tells you, "Come over here. Talk to this person." "I can't talk to this person." You learn to obey. If you do as He tells you, you will become very sensitive to the Spirit of God. Learn to

7

obey and learn how to take a stand for God, and God will bless you.

Learn His Word Where did Elijah get this boldness to say, "It's not going to rain for three years"? Would you dare to go to a king or a president and say, "You better repent or it's not going to rain for three years"? Where did Elijah get this from? He got it from Deuteronomy 11:16-17:

> Beware, lest your hearts be deceived and you turn away and serve other gods and worship them. Or the anger of the LORD will be kindled against you, and He will shut up the heavens so that there will be no rain and the ground will not yield its fruit; and you will perish quickly from the good land which the LORD is giving you.

Elijah knew this Scripture. He knew God's commands and God's warnings and he just applied them. You can learn the Word of God and learn to apply it, too.

Take a stand for God. You see somebody in sin. How do you know it is sin? You know it, because you know the Word of God. You can take a stand for God against that sin by telling the brother, "You better repent." Brothers and sisters, learn the Word of God, develop a lifestyle of obedience, and you will be ready for anything God tells you to do. Are you excited about the vitality of God? Do you know that you are God's personal representative? Are you developing a lifestyle of obedience? Are you ready to take a stand for God?

The Deterrents

Secret obedience It is hard for many of us as it was hard for the people of Elijah's day. Three years had gone by when we come to chapter eighteen. There had been many miracles in Elijah's life, and now it was the time for Elijah to come face to face with Ahab. In verse three, Ahab called his servant Obadiah. In the parentheses, the Bible says:

Obadiah feared the LORD greatly. (1 Ki. 18:3)

The Bible wants us to know that Obadiah was a man of God, although he was a servant of a wicked king. Deep down inside he really feared the Lord greatly. In fact, he took a hundred prophets, hid them by fifties in two caves, and provided them with bread and water (v. 4). As a result, a hundred prophets were still alive. Later on, we find out that 7,000 prophets were still alive, hiding in caves to give their silent protest. They did not like what king Ahab was doing, but they stayed in their caves to give their silent protest.

Many Christians are doing that today. Oh, they obey the Lord, but it is a kind of secret obedience. "I really fear the Lord." But, it is a secret fear. "I don't want to come out to the public." "I am afraid for my life." "I don't want people to laugh at me." "I don't like what's happening." "I don't like injustice." "I don't like sins." But all we do is talk among ourselves in a cave. We are hiding in our churches. We take no stand for God. We can talk about the world in the Church, but outside the Church we take no stand for God.

There are things wrong in this government, yet we never write a letter to our congressman. Some of us are not even registered to vote, and we are citizens of the United States. We do not take our responsibilities seriously. Although we are Christians, we take no stand for God nor for righteousness; we never speak out. That will never do. "We're Chinese. We're reserved. We don't get involved in those kinds of things." We are Chinese and we have our culture. That is true, but we are Christians too! Christians need to stand up for God, whether we are Chinese or not. It is our right, it is our duty and it is our responsibility. Take a stand for God. Do not hide in caves!

Double-mindedness After the great battle on Mount Carmel, Elijah asked the people of Israel:

> "How long will you hesitate between two opinions? If the LORD is God, follow Him; but if Baal, follow him." (1 Ki. 18:21)

The people had two opinions. They were following God and they were following Baal. It was not that they forsook the Lord God. They kept Him, but they wanted Baal worship too. They wanted a little bit of both worlds.

Are not many Christians doing that today? They are double-minded. They will never forsake God. They come to church, and they go to prayer meeting perhaps. "Don't ask me to sacrifice my life. I don't want to take up my cross." "I still like riches." "I still want to be someone in the world." "I want to cling on to God, but I want to go after other things too." That will never do. With a double mind, we will never stand for God. Elijah shouts it out to you and to me, "How long are you going to do this?"

There was a very sad commentary at the end of verse twenty-one: "But the people did not answer him a word." They would not make a decision. You and I need to make a decision to be single-minded. This was why Jesus condemned the church of Laodicea—they were neither cold nor hot; they were lukewarm! They said, "Oh! we're rich. We have need of nothing." But Jesus said:

> you do not know that you are wretched and miserable and poor and blind and naked.... (Rev. 3:17)

They kicked Jesus out the door. Jesus came back knocking on the door, saying:

if any one hears My voice and opens the door, I will come
in to him.... (Rev. 3:20)

It is a sad thing. This church was carrying out its program, its
worship service, its prayer meeting and its fellowship groups,
but Jesus was outside the door. It was functioning beautifully,
but there was no Holy Spirit inside. That is very sad. That can
happen! A church can be doing just fine without God, because
there are too many worldly ambitions. A double-minded
attitude will prevent us from taking a stand for God.

Wrong priority In order to stand for God, we have to
know who our God is. How do we know who our God is?
Verse twenty-one tells us: Our God is the one we follow.
Whom or what do we follow? If we follow the business news
and the stock market and if we read that more than the Bible,
we are following riches. Then, simply, that is our god. Trying
to hang on to the true God while actually following another is
double-mindedness. We need to be single-minded and follow
the true God.

I really praise the Lord last week that I preached over at
our Westminster Branch Church. When I was sitting in the
office before the service, I overheard two brothers talking. One
brother was saying, "I don't think we should have visitation
next week." The other asked, "Why?" "Well, the Super Bowl
football game will be on television next Sunday. Not too many
people are going to go." I really chuckled under my breath,
because I was going to preach on visitation. So, when I got up
to the pulpit, I really hammered on visitation. I was not
planning to emphasize it that much, but since the Lord allowed
me to hear this comment, I thought He wanted me to preach on
it. They told me that forty-five people signed up for visitation
and that was the most people they ever had. I praise God for
the victory.

There is nothing wrong in watching the Super Bowl on television. I love to watch it myself, but I do not want to miss worship by watching the Super Bowl! There are priorities. There are people who have needs, and there are things we have to do for God. We need to be trained to arrange our priorities. Can you take a stand for God? You cannot do so if you are double-minded. Whom do you follow? Do you follow sports? If so, sports is your god. It is that simple.

False sincerity Look at the cults today. They keep Jesus Christ, but they add other things too. They look like Christianity, don't they? I just heard someone who was formerly involved with the Mormons, testify on the radio that it took him two years to realize that Mormonism was not a Christian faith. He was stuck in there for two years. Cults pose as Christianity. We do not doubt the sincerity of these people. In fact, these people who worshipped Baal cried out from morning till noon (1 Ki. 18:26). When there was no answer, they leaped upon the altar, jumped on the altar and cried with a loud voice for over three hours (v. 28) ! They even slashed their wrists until their blood gushed out on their sacrifice. Of course they were sincere. But sincerity does not mean that they had the truth. Better remember that! There are a lot of sincere and good people in other religions. The Mormons are good people; the Jehovah's Witnesses are good people. They are sincere in what they believe. The problem is that they believe in the wrong thing. That is the true test.

What is truth then? The objective truth of Jesus Christ is the resurrection. Look at the people who follow the cults and those who are involved in spiritism. There is a spiritual poverty among these people. They are looking for the truth of Christian faith, but they cannot see the reality of God. Why? It is because no one takes a stand for God. There were 450 prophets of Baal and 400 prophets of other false gods. There was only one prophet of the true God. But that can make all the difference in the world. To have one true Christian who stands for God can turn this whole generation to Jesus Christ.

The Manifestations

How do we take a stand for God? In 1 Kings 18:30, Elijah said to all the people:

"Come near to me."

That is taking a stand for God. You are not afraid for people to come near to you. Make your faith public. Do not keep such a secret obedience. It is all right for people to see. Invite people to come and see. Give a clear demonstration of your stand for God.

Repair your altar What did Elijah do? He repaired the altar of the Lord, which had been torn down (1 Ki. 18:30). What is an altar? An altar is where you worship and where you sacrifice. Has the altar in your heart been torn down? You do not truly worship anymore. You do not worship at home. You do not sacrifice your life. You are not serving the Lord. Something tore it down! The world tore it down, or you tore it down yourself, or some friends tore it down. Take a stand for God! Repair the altar of the Lord. Get back to true worship. Make it public. People see you go to church—so what? Let people see you say grace at lunch time. Invite them to see. Sacrifice your life, and serve the Lord. It is not easy to take a stand for God, but we need to do it.

I was recently struck with the truth: God is so big that I cannot understand all of Him. I cannot comprehend His infinity, and I cannot get hold of who He is. But God has not called me to understand Him, or to get a hold of Him in my hand. God has not called me to do that. What God has called me to do is to worship Him. I cannot understand all of Him, but I can worship Him, love Him and adore Him. That is what you and I are called to do. Repair the altar of the Lord. Get back to true worship. Be faithful in public attendance and in private worship. Take a stand for the Lord.

God will burn wet wood In 1 Kings 18:33-34, Elijah prayed and then water was poured over the sacrifice. Wait a minute. You cannot burn wet wood! You cannot burn wet wood, but when you take a stand for the Lord you can watch God burn wet wood. That is exactly what God did. You cannot burn wet wood! "I cannot be a pastor." "I cannot be a missionary." "I cannot teach the Word of God." "I cannot serve Him in church." "God, you can't burn wet wood." Brothers and sisters, you are all wet, but God can burn in you. Take a stand for God and watch Him burn the wet wood.

People will know God Why do we need to take a stand? The great prayer of Elijah in verse thirty-seven shows us the reasons why we need to take a stand for God:

> "Answer me, O LORD, answer me, that this people
> may know that Thou, O LORD, art God, and that Thou
> hast turned their heart back again."

When we take a stand for God, people will see the reality and the vitality of God in our lives, and then they will come to know the Lord. Secondly, people will know that God will turn their hearts back again. You and I need to take a stand for God for these reasons. When you take a stand for God, people will know who God is and will know that God wants to turn their hearts back.

Let me tell you a true story that happened in a church. There was a young man who loved the Lord and wanted to get baptized. His father was vehemently against it and said, "If you get baptized, you will be sorry." But the young man loved the Lord so much that he wanted to follow Him in baptism, so

TAKING A STAND FOR GOD

he got baptized. When his father knew it, he confronted him and slapped him. The son fell to the ground, and said, "Father, I love you, but I love the Lord more." The father hit him again. Blood began coming out from his mouth. "Father I love you, but I love the Lord Jesus too." The father hit him again and repeatedly hit him. The son kept saying, "I love you, father, but I love the Lord too." When the father was about to hit him again, suddenly it dawned upon the father and he asked himself, "What am I doing?" He saw his son all battered and bruised. It convicted his heart so much. Later, the father came to know Christ, and he himself got baptized.

Take a stand for God. I am not advocating for young people to disobey their parents. But with wisdom and wise discretion, sometimes we need to take a stand. When we take a stand, people will see that there must be something to our God. Are you taking a stand for Him? He is valuable. If you do not take those stands, they do not know that your God is worth standing for. When you do it, people will know the true God, and will know that God wants to turn their hearts back to Him. Oh, take a stand for God! It is important. Is it important? It is important! Let us take a stand for God.

15

TAKE HOLD OF ETERNAL LIFE

If I were to ask you what the fundamental need of a man was, what would your answer be? Some of you might think that, "Well, a man needs food and water." That is certainly good for his physical needs. "A man needs security." "He needs love." "He needs to know that he belongs." And you might give all kinds of answers. Psychologists have tried to think of these things, but the basic need of Man has not really been answered. That is the answer to death. Philosophers and different religions try to give an answer to death; nevertheless, there is always the quest for immortality—the fountain of youth. Nobody wants to die. We all want to live. To maintain our life is, therefore, the real need for us. But how can we do that? For alas, we know that people die and that, one day, it will happen to you and to me.

Understanding Eternal Life

The great scientist Sir Michael Faraday was a Christian. Those of you who study electricity or electrolysis will know his name. As he was dying, some journalists came and asked him his speculations concerning life after death. This great scientist gave his answer and said, "Speculations? I know of no speculations! I am resting on certainties, for I know that my Redeemer lives, and because He lives I shall live also."

Years ago, the great evangelist, D. L. Moody talked to his friend, "Some day you will read in the newspaper that D. L. Moody is dead. Don't believe a word of it, for at that moment, I shall be more alive than I've ever been. I was born in 1837, but I was born of the Spirit in 1856. That which was born of the flesh may die, but that which was born of the Spirit may live forever." Are you not glad? I am! I am so glad that our faith rests on certainties, not on speculations, because we have the truth of the resurrection of Jesus Christ. Jesus literally and historically died, and He literally and historically rose again from the grave. That is a manifestation of the truth of eternal life. If we would put our faith and trust in Him, we would not perish but have eternal life. There is more to eternal life than we normally think.

The temporal life

a. A divine gift Let us turn to 1 Timothy chapter six. Here we see some practical aspects about eternal life. The word "life" is mentioned three times in this passage. The first time is in verse thirteen:

> I charge you in the presence of God, who gives life to all things . . . .

This "life" is the life God gives. Anything and everything you see around you, that has life, has its life from God. It is the general life every creature has and it is from God. It is a wonderful gift; it is a holy gift; it is precious to us; and it is from God.

That is why we need to stand against abortion. The issue

of abortion is not—"Is that embryo or that fetus really a human being?" That is not the issue! Neither is it a theological issue—"Does that embryo or that fetus have a soul yet?" or "at what age, or after how many weeks or how many months, is that embryo a human being?" That is not the issue! That embryo, that fetus, or whatever you want to call it has life, even if it is just a mass of tissue in its early stage. When you take a little bit out of it, you can see the cells. It has life, and life is from God. God is the one who gives life to all things. Your life is from God too. So, you should never seek to take your own life, because your life is good, your life is holy and your life is from God.

b. A destined death Let us turn to Ecclesiastes 2:14-16:

> The wise man's eyes are in his head, but the fool walks in darkness. And yet I know that one fate befalls them both. Then I said to myself, "As is the fate of the fool, it will also befall me. Why then have I been extremely wise?" So I said to myself, "This too is vanity." For there is no lasting remembrance of the wise man as with the fool, inasmuch as in the coming days all will be forgotten. And how the wise man and the fool alike die!

Are you a wise man or are you a foolish one? It makes no difference in the end. You spend all your time going to school to get your advance degrees. What difference does it make? One day, you and all fools will die, and you will be forgotten. So, why do you strive to be a fool or a wise man? Look at Ecclesiastes 3:19, then you will see the difference between a man and an animal. There is no difference either: As an animal will die, so will a man die.

Ecclesiastes 5:15-16 talk about a man who works unceasingly trying to attain wealth. What good is it? He is going to die someday and he cannot take any accumulation of his riches with him. So, why then do you work so hard? You are toiling in the wind that blows your work away. You know that this is reality and you know that it is true: One day you will die. Why should you work so hard? Why should you strive to be wise? Whether you are a fool, whether you are a wise man, whether you are poor or whether you are rich, it makes no difference. We sense the temporal condition of Man.

c. An eternal perspective We see in Ecclesiastes 3:11 another condition of Man. It says:

> He has made everything appropriate in its time. He has also
> set eternity in their heart . . . .

When we consider our lives, we sense not only a temporal status but also an eternal status. I really sense that there has to be something more than this life. "Is there a life after death?" There is the eternity in our hearts. We have a sense of judgment, because we sense that one day we will be accountable to a God for all the things we have done. We have guilty feelings, because we feel that one day we have to stand before a judge. We have a sense of morality of what is right and what is wrong. That is the eternity in our hearts. There ought to be something more than just this life, for we sense that what we are going through today is in preparation for something in the future. These eternal and temporal perspectives in our lives bring so much confusion that we begin to philosophize and theologize in trying to find an answer. This is the life God gives to us, but we get so confused about it.

The eternal life As we look back at 1 Timothy chapter six, we see the second mention of "life" in verse twelve:

> Fight the good fight of faith; take hold of the eternal life....

There is not only a life in general but also a life eternal. Here the Bible speaks of eternal life as something concrete, something you can take hold of. This eternal life came when God called you: You heard the message of Jesus Christ, you responded and you received Him into your heart. When you gave a public testimony or a confession in front of many witnesses, that was the confirmation of your eternal life. This happens at your baptism. Before you get baptized, you give a public testimony. How good it is when the witnesses confirm that you are saved and that you have eternal life. This is where eternal life begins: If you receive Jesus Christ into your heart, you are a Christian and you have eternal life. But it is not good enough just to have eternal life, you have to take hold of it.

The word "life" is mentioned the third time in verse nineteen:

> storing up for themselves the treasure of a good foundation
> for the future, so that they may take hold of that which is
> life indeed.

This is the future aspect of "life." Eternal life is a present possession you take hold of for the future life indeed. The same idea is found in Mark 10:30, where Jesus is talking about the reward given to those who follow Him:

> but that he shall receive a hundred times as much now in the
> present age, houses and brothers and sisters and mothers and
> children and farms, along with persecutions; and in the age to
> come, eternal life.

You see, you get many wonderful blessings in this present life; however, there may be persecutions and bad things as well. But, "in the age to come," it will be eternal life! Eternal life has more meanings than you and I normally think. There are at least four meanings of eternal life.

a. A life living unto eternity Firstly, it means "to live forever." The word "eternal" means forever, an ageless duration of time. If you really have eternal life, you should have no fear of death. If you are a Christian and you are afraid to die, you are immature. If you have eternal life, as you grow in the Lord, you will take hold of it and you will not fear death, for the life God gives you is eternal.

b. A life having God's quality Secondly, eternal life means the very life of God Himself. God has eternal life. If you have eternal life, there should be a new quality of life in you. God is good, merciful and love. These qualities should be seen in your life. There should be a new quality in your life: the quality of the very life of God Himself. The Bible says that this life is in His Son:

> He who has the Son has life; he who does not have the Son of God does not have the life. (1 Jn. 5:12)

c. A life knowing the Almighty The third meaning of eternal life is found in John 17:3:

> And this is eternal life, that they may know Thee, the only true God, and Jesus Christ whom Thou hast sent.

Not only is eternal life living forever, not only is it the very life of God Himself, but also it is knowing God. The word "knowing" is a progressive knowing, to know God better and better. Knowing is a relationship. You have a relationship with God—a personal relationship which calls for interaction with God. The higher your interaction is, the higher the form of life will be. A worm interacts with its environment, and all it interacts with is the soil. When a man interacts with his environment, he interacts with other people, but he also can interact with the highest God Himself. That is the higher form of life. Eternal life is knowing God, a relationship of the highest caliber. If you really have eternal life you should be knowing God better and better. You should be praying more, reading your Bible more, and going to church to fellowship and worship more, for you have a dynamic, active and personal relationship with God. Eternal life means you know Him and you are knowing Him more and more.

d. A life entering the Kingdom The fourth meaning of eternal life is in Matthew 19:16. This is the incident of Jesus talking with the rich young ruler who wanted to know how he could get eternal life. He asked Jesus, "Teacher, what good thing shall I do that I may obtain eternal life?" Jesus said, "but if you wish to enter into life . . ." (Mt. 19:17). What does it mean by "to enter into life"? In verse twenty-three Jesus said:

> Truly I say to you, it is hard for a rich man to enter the kingdom of heaven.

"To enter into life" is to enter into the Kingdom. As I have said before, life has a future aspect to it. It is life indeed—it is the life you and I are striving for; it is the life we are hoping for.

So, if you truly have eternal life, there should be four things happening:

1. You should not worry about death, for you will live forever.
2. You should have a new quality in your life: Your thinking, your attitude and your behavior should all be shaping into conformity with the standard of God.
3. You should have an active relationship with God.
4. You should be moving toward the Kingdom.

Living Eternal Life

From having to entering Eternal life comes when you receive Jesus Christ. To have eternal life is not enough, as that is only the beginning. Now that you have eternal life, the goal is to enter into life. How do you make the transition from having eternal life to entering into eternal life? The transition is to take hold of eternal life. When you take hold of eternal life, you will enter into eternal life. You already have it, and you must take hold of it. The Bible says in Revelation 3:11:

> hold fast what you have, in order that no one take your crown.

You can lose your crown if you do not take hold of eternal life—which you already have.

From entering to living Maybe you have an understanding about eternal life, but there is a difference between entering into eternal life and living eternal life. I am surprised that so many Christians who have eternal life do not know how to live it. I have heard so many people say, "I don't want to become a Christian, because if I do, I won't have fun anymore." Shame on us that we are modeling the Christian life as something that has no fun. If we have eternal life, we should be having the most fun that we ever had in our lives. God has given us life to enjoy; yet we think that to be a Christian, we have to show a sour face, to walk around with our hands folded and our heads bowed all the time, and to have a look of piety with a frown on our face.

I have heard so many Christian girls complain, "We go out with the guys from this church and our dates are so boring." Our brothers do not know how to have fun or how to enjoy a date or even a marriage. They are boring. They do not know how to live. God calls us to live our eternal life which is for now as well as for the future. Take hold of it now!

Taking Hold of Eternal Life

Satan is trying to put all kinds of snares and traps in our way. He knows that he cannot take away the eternal life we have already possessed, but he will throw obstacles trying to prevent us from taking hold of what we already have.

Therefore, I will give you three important points to take hold of eternal life.

Develop the strategy for living

a. Respond to things of life Let us go to 1 Timothy chapter six. Firstly, we must develop the strategy for living. Quit having such a dull life. The Lord has given us a Christian life full of joy, so we should be able to respond immediately to things in life. In our eternal life, God has given us a creative mind. You just sit there and pray about it. Then, you will find out that God has given you a creative mind. As you grow in the Lord, you will be able to respond, you will know how to have fun, and you will know how to enjoy life.

One time, I heard a preacher talking about the assassination attempt on President Reagan. He said, "You remember the newsreel about the shooting attempt on the President. How immediately the secret servicemen surrounded the President, sealing him with their bodies. What a fast reaction those secret servicemen had!" And he continued, "Of course, you know that those secret servicemen are not Christians. How do you know they're not Christians? If they were Christians, when they heard the shot, they would first of all hold a prayer meeting. They would have a board meeting and take a vote before doing what they should do." That is a shame if that is true! If we are Christians, we should be able to respond immediately, and we should know how to live. But, it takes some growing up though.

b. Pursue things of eternal life Look at the strategy the Lord gives here in 1 Timothy 6:11. The Bible says that we have to flee and we have to pursue. What do we flee from? Verse nine talks about those who want to get rich. We have to flee from the temptation of going after riches. Note very carefully that Paul is not talking to the rich people, but

25

rather, he is talking to the one who wants to get rich. He is talking to you and to me. There are all kinds of snares and foolish desires which plunge men into ruin and destruction. There is nothing evil about the riches and possessions we have. What the Bible says here is that the love of money and the attitude toward money will lead us to all sorts of evil. Of course we need money and we need sound investment to take care of our family. But there are those who go to the other extremes, and those who want fame and fortune which lead to moral decay. We have to flee from those things and pursue

> righteousness, godliness, faith, love, perseverance and gentleness. (1 Tim. 6:11)

Let these virtues be your objectives for living. Whatever you are facing in life, let these virtues come to mind. Think of the presence of the Lord. Do not go after the things of the world, because they are not things of eternal life. Life is not measured by the amount of things and possessions you have. So strive for the qualities of virtues and the kind of person you ought to be. If you do that, you will know how to live. Do not chase after worldly things; do not chase after riches or popularity; just be quiet. But pursue, and always pursue, and keep on pursuing the things that are good. If you do that, you will grow, you will have a purity of life and you will know how to live.

How can a Christian have fun? A Christian can joke around. We need a balance in our life. There are times we are serious, but there are times to laugh and times to joke around in purity, in righteousness, in love and in gentleness. Our Lord will teach us how to live. Before you can pursue these things, you have to flee from those other things.

Determine the standards for winning Secondly, determine the standards for winning. If you want to take hold of eternal life, you better learn how to live and learn how to fight. Before you can fight, you better know that you are going to win. People play games because they think that they are going to win. You will never play a game thinking, "Oh I'm going to play because I am going to lose." Each of you Christians here ought to know that he is a winner and he is going to win. There will be struggles and there will be difficulties, but at the end there will be victory. 1 Timothy 6:14-16 say that the King of kings and Lord of lords is going to come. He is the one who will bring us victory. You are a winner, and you need to have that in your mind.

    a. ***Have a good fight*** How are you going to be a winner? You have to know that you will have a good fight (1 Tim. 6:12). Do you not just love to get into a good fight? But, too many Christians back away. They do not want to get involved; they have lost sight of how to win and how to take hold of eternal life. Do not be afraid to get your feet wet, because this is a good fight. The word "good" means "excellent." And the word "fight" is the Greek word a̅go̅nia ἀγωνία (fight), from which we get the word "agony," a struggle. A Christian's life is not going to be easy. Oh, but it is going to be fulfilling! It is going to make uphill fighting hard! You must have the attitude that you can win. If you know that you are going to win, you will know that you are going to have a good fight and you will not give up. Serve the Lord—get in there, roll up your sleeves and get to work! Do not be afraid. Share your faith. People may ridicule you, but it is a good fight. Take hold of eternal life, and fight the good fight of faith. Make it the best fight.

    b. ***Get charged before God*** How are you going to be a winner? In 1 Timothy 6:13 the Bible says:

> I charge you in the presence of God . . . .

You have to get charged in the presence of God. You and I need more charges. We have to hear more preaching, go to more retreats and camps, and hear more speakers. I hope that in your car you have your button preset on one of the Christian radio stations. You need to listen to some of the stations where famous preachers, like Billy Graham, are preaching. You need to get charged in the presence of God. The more charges you get, the more sure a winner you will be. When you get charged up, you will know what to do. You will get motivated, and you will be ready to take hold of eternal life and to fight the good fight of faith.

Discover the secrets of giving

a. Do not give way Do not give way to the Devil. He will try to get you sidetracked. Therefore, you need to be single-minded and you need to know how to live. Do not give way!

b. Do not give up Do not give up. There will be discouragements, but you are a winner. Fight the good fight of faith. Do not give up! Do not give way; do not give up.

c. Do give The Bible says in 1 Timothy 6:17:

> Instruct those who are rich in this present world not to be conceited . . . .

Rich is a relative term. You can always find somebody richer than you and someone poorer than you. Let us face it, brothers and sisters. We live in this rich country; we are rich. So this verse is for you and for me. The Bible says that to instruct them not to be conceited. "Conceited" means high-minded and proud. They fixed their hopes on the uncertainties of riches.

Do you always spend your time reading the newspaper stock market exchange? Do you always look at your bank account and always worry about the interest rates? Where is your hope? Is your hope in riches? Is your hope in the economy? Or, do you fix your hope in God? "Fixing" is to concentrate. Where is the major thrust of your concentration? It needs to be on God, not on the uncertainties of riches. If you concentrate on riches, you are proud and you are conceited. Why does God make any one rich? Do you want to know why God gives you a lot of money? Why does God let you have extra money in your pocket right now? God does so that you can give it away, and that you can help others who have needs.

Then the Bible continues to say in verse eighteen:

> Instruct them to do good, to be rich in good works, to be generous and ready to share . . . .

God wants you to be generous. The words "to be generous" come from the Greek word koinōnia κοινωνία (fellowship), which means fellowship. It is not just depositing money on people's laps but also fellowshipping. That means your heart is involved. You give not just your money but also your heart. Be rich not in money but in good works. That is how you take hold of eternal life.

- Do not give way to sidetracks.
- Do not give up.
- Do give.

If you do that, verse nineteen tells us that your future is secure. You will take hold of that which is life indeed. You have eternal life. Good! But that is just the beginning. You need to take hold of it and have a firm grasp of it. Learn how to live, learn how to win, and learn how to give. Take hold of your eternal life and you will enter into life.

HOW PERSONAL IS YOUR GOD?

One of the most common difficulties a Christian has is to know the personal presence of God. "Intellectually and theologically I seem to know that God is here, but practically speaking I don't feel the presence of God." This is the complaint of many Christians. God seems so far away that we do not sense His closeness. "I feel like a hypocrite because I sit in church thinking 'Where's God?' But at the same time I'll never leave God. I need God—I have fears and dangers in my life, and I don't know what will happen to me in the future—but I don't feel God."

Christians are in this dilemma where they want to have God but they do not feel God. It is a continual dilemma for many. Going to church then becomes a ritual and a habit. Even relationships with other Christians become trite and meaningless. They are very polite to one another, but really, they are indifferent to becoming intimately involved in each other's life. If this is the state of the Church, we are in trouble.

We have to tell the world that God is here. If we do not know it, how is the world going to know it? So we need to be reminded again of the closeness of our God and of the relationship we have with Him.

His Perception of Me

I would like us to turn to Psalm 139. As we read this beautiful Hebrew poem and as we study and understand it, we will see that God is very personal. It is vital for us to grab hold of this truth; otherwise, God will be so far away for the rest of our lives. There are four stanzas in this Psalm and each has six verses. They are beautifully descriptive of our God.

He is involved We begin with verse one:

> O LORD, Thou hast searched me and known me.

The psalmist begins right away with how personal God is. In fact, when we look at the verbs in these few verses, we will see how God knows you and me: "He searches me; He knows me." He knows when I sit down and when I rise up. He understands my thoughts. In verse three, He scrutinizes my path, and He is intimately acquainted with all my ways. God KNOWS me. He has searched me, and the search and the knowledge are complete. There never was a time He did not know me. He has always known me, and He has always known you. There never was a time He did not know you. This is our God. He is involved with our lives.

a. He knows my actions He knows when I sit down and He knows when I rise up. When we think of "sitting" and "standing," we know that they are common things we do everyday. There is nothing special about them, but the Lord is interested! From this we see that God takes notice of the most casual actions we do. He is never bored; He is never indifferent. The Lord knows us. I sit down because I am tired; or I sit down to think about a question, to ponder on something; or I sit down when I am depressed and discouraged. The Lord knows. The Lord knows when I rise up. When I rise up, maybe, I am going to move; or I am going to take action; or I am going to take a walk. The Lord knows.

b. ***He knows my thoughts*** My thoughts, He understands. Verse two says that He understands them "from afar." He knows my thoughts even before I formulate my own thoughts. He knows what I am thinking even before I know it. The Lord knows everything about me. He knows me better than I know myself. God is never surprised. We never find God saying, "GASP!!!" He is never surprised. I may do something on the spur of the moment spontaneously, but He knows already. The Lord knows me—He knows my path, He knows my lying down, and He knows every intricate detail of my life. He has done research on me and He is involved with every area, even the most casual activities, of my life. He is totally interested in me.

c. ***To know myself better*** He knows me better than I know myself. If that is true, it stands to reason, then, that if I know my God better, I will know myself better. I know my sons better than they know themselves. I know their moods, their emotions and when they are tired. They do not like me to tell them to take a nap. But I know them better than they know themselves. The beautiful times are when we, my children and I, can sit down, and I can talk about their lives and what I know about them. They then begin to see that I know them better than they know themselves. God knows us better than we know ourselves. What beautiful times there are when we can sit and talk with God, get to know Him better and consequently get to know ourselves better. Therefore, if I become intimately involved with my God, I will begin to know myself intimately.

d. To know others better It also stands to reason that when I become intimately involved with my personal God, I will also become more intimately involved with God's people. For the Bible tells us that if we say we love God and hate our brother, we are liars (1 Jn. 4:20). The one who loves God is the one who loves his brother. So many of us have problems loving one another. Oh, we might talk, and when we see each other along the way we might say, "Hello"; but we are afraid to get intimately involved in each other's life, basically because we ourselves have a lot of fears and a lot of insecurities. These are things we do not want other people to know about. But when we get to know our personal God who knows everything about us, and when we become intimate with Him, we learn to become intimate with people. It is difficult for some of us to relate to people, because we do not know how to relate to God. When we get to know God, we will get to know ourselves better. So, if we have difficulty with some people, we need to get back to God.

He is Intimate In verse six, the psalmist says:

> Such knowledge is too wonderful for me;
> It is too high, I cannot attain to it.

God knows me in such detail. This is really too wonderful and too hard for me to conceive: God knows every detail of my life, yet He still loves me. It is a humbling experience, isn't it? He knows my bad side as well as my good side, yet He still loves me. It is too wonderful for me to grasp. God loves you too. When you know your God, you will be excited. You will never lose the wonder but will be constantly saying, "WOW."

His Presence with Me

We see in the first stanza that the Lord's omniscience is always with us. If His omniscience is there, then His omnipresence is there also.

At all locations   The psalmist says in the second stanza:

> Where can I go from Thy Spirit?
> Or where can I flee from Thy presence?
> If I ascend to heaven, Thou art there;

We cannot go any higher. The Lord is there. "If I make my bed in Sheol, behold, Thou art there."   Verse nine says:

> If I take the wings of the dawn,
> If I dwell in the remotest part of the sea,

Have you ever gotten up to see the sunrise in the morning? The sun slowly comes up over the horizon in the east. As soon as it breaks through, the rays of light stream across the horizon. If you could sit on one of those rays, you would swiftly go through the atmosphere at the speed of light. If I could sit on the rays, if I could take the wings of dawn with its swiftness and quickness, or if I could dwell way out there, far away in the sea, in the remotest part of the sea, and in the vast expansion of loneliness, "even there, Thy hand will lead me." We can go to the highest heavens, we can go to the depths of Sheol, and, we can go as swift as the rays of light and as vast as the universe; yet, behold, the Lord is there! Not only is He there, but He also takes an active part in leading us.

In all situations   When we think that darkness is overwhelming, yet we know as in verse twelve that:

> Even the darkness is not dark to Thee,
> And the night is as bright as the day.
> Darkness and light are alike to Thee.

God penetrates the dark, for God is light and in Him there is no darkness (1 Jn. 1:5). That is why it says in the book of Revelation that there is no darkness in the Kingdom of God: "there shall no longer be any night; . . . because the Lord God shall illumine them. . ." (Rev. 22:5). Our God is not in our realm of dimension. He is in His own sphere and He can penetrate our dimension. Nothing controls our God, but our God is, in fact, in control. So God is not controlled by any dimension, but He is the one who controls the dimensions.

Filled with joy　God is with us. I do not see this as an oppressive measure, or as "I can't do it because God is always looking over my shoulder." Oh, no! I see God's presence with me as a source of joy and an answer to loneliness. Have you ever felt lonely? Even though you are sitting at church with lots of people, yet you feel like you are alone. Or, maybe, you are in despair and discouragement. Nobody cares; nobody can help. But God is present. He is our personal God. He knows who we are and He will be with us in any situation and at any location: at the heights and at the depths; at good times and at bad times.

Filled with sensitivity　Then, it also stands to reason that as you and I get to know this personal God, we will become sensitive to lonely people, because we know that God is with us. He is always with us and He is with other people too. His presence is with God's people. When we become sensitive to that, we will begin to spot those who are sitting by themselves, and we can sense that there is something wrong with somebody even when he is talking and joking around. We become very sensitive to people who do not know that God is with them. When we know our God in a personal way, we want to share. God is with us no matter what the dimension is; God is there.

His Power upon Me

In making me　The third stanza, in verses thirteen and fourteen, says:

For Thou didst form my inward parts;
Thou didst weave me in my mother's womb.
I will give thanks to Thee, for I am fearfully and
   wonderfully made;

Here, the psalmist is proclaiming how wonderfully he is made. Can you proclaim that? This is not an issue of pride, but a matter of thanksgiving. He is thankful for the way he is made. The Lord has worked even before we were born. Verse sixteen says, "Thine eyes have seen my unformed substance." This is talking about when you and I were a "blob" in our mother's womb. The Lord was actively involved in the shaping of the embryo. It took time for the Lord to shape it up. It took nine months before we were born. God was intricately involved with the details of our making.

I do not know if you have ever studied the structure of a cell, the biochemistry, the enzyme reactions, and all the things that are happening in one cell. There are millions of those cells in us. We have different organs with different functions: the heart, the brain, the eye, the ear, the mouth... The Lord has made us. We are to be thankful. I wonder if you are thankful.

In leading me If we know our personal God, we will know that He was involved with our making. All that time, all that energy and all that power were put into the making of each of us. Do you know what that tells us? It tells us that we are of infinite worth to God. God has spent all that effort to make us, because He counts us to be worthy. He has a purpose for each of our lives. He would not have spent all that time, and done all that engineering and all that designing if He did not have a plan for us.

a. Consider God's plan We are of infinite worth to God and yet, as you know, we are not all the same. We do not

37

look alike; sometimes we do not think alike. We are individuals. God would make a baby the same way, but we come out different. In verse sixteen, it says how

> And in Thy book they were all written,
> The days that were ordained for me,

Even before the baby has one day, his/her whole life has already been plotted out and written in the book. Oh, the Lord loves us. He has spent so much time and effort to make us. It is not without purpose. God invested all that power in us because He has a plan for us, and His plan is written in the book.

Now, you and I have a choice. God has not made us to be robots; we do not have to follow that plan. If we want, we can choose plan B, or plan C, or any other plan we like. But let us have an understanding right now about plan A. The plan God has made is the very best one for our lives, because God has designed us for the very purpose of fitting that plan. Any other plan we take just will not fit perfectly. We are designed with certain specifications: our physical and psychological make-up. God made us and He did not make a mistake. God invites you and me to walk according to His plan for our individual lives.

b. Accept God's creation I am of infinite worth and you are too. There is no mistake in how we look today. We may not like our nose; our feet may be too big; our lips may be too fat; our ears may be too flappy; and we may wish to be skinnier. A certain feature that is ugly in one particular culture may be a point of beauty in another. In the American culture people like skinny women, but in another culture, like Mexico, they like plump women. God made us who we are. When we know our personal God, we will be able to accept who we are. We are special. God spent all His effort and energy to make us who we are today.

Verse seventeen says, "How precious also are Thy thoughts to me, O God! / How vast is the sum of them!" God has special precious thoughts toward us. If we would count them all, they would outnumber the sand. Have you ever gone to a beach to take a handful of sand, and tried to count all the grains? That is only a handful. Take a whole beach, Huntington Beach or Newport Beach, and count all those grains of sand. The precious thoughts of God toward us outnumber them; God loves us. We are of infinite worth to Him. We are special. Praise the Lord!

His Protection of Me

We know that God knows who we are. He is always with us, and He is very interested in us. He has spent all His power and energy and time to make us who we are, because He has a plan for each of our lives. And it stands to reason that if He spent all that time and energy to make us for the plan, He would protect us so that we can do the plan.

From the wickedness without In verse nineteen we see the cry against the wicked. As God's people, we are never to be naive of the wickedness of this world. We Christians are not like those people who just lie back, respond passively and even let the wicked people walk all over them. We are to separate ourselves from wickedness. We see in the psalmist a single-minded zeal for God. Because he loves his God so much and because he knows his personal God, a hatred for wickedness is created in him.

Of course we are to be compassionate to all men. But when we have such a zeal for God and when God is really first in our lives, our love for God, in comparison to other relationships, looks like hatred towards other people. The Lord Jesus even told us that in the New Testament:

> He who loves father or mother more than Me is not worthy
> of Me. . . . (Mt. 10:37)

He said that we have to hate our father and mother, wife and children and brothers and sisters (Lk. 14:26). It does not mean "to hate" them literally, but because we have such a zeal for the Lord, our love for our loved ones, in comparison, looks like hatred. Do you have such single-mindedness towards God? We will have it when we get to know our God better and when He really is our personal God. If we get to know the Lord and have this zeal, we will be very, very sensitive to wicked things.

Many of us are too involved with worldly things, and many things we do as Christians are questionable. We are afraid to draw lines between ourselves and the world. But, when we have a zeal for God and when God becomes personal in our lives, we will be very sensitive to wicked things and we will not want to do them. God will answer our prayers and protect us from the wicked things of this world.

From the wickedness within   But there is also a wickedness within. We need the Lord to show us the wickedness within and protect us from ourselves, our flesh. Compare verse twenty-three with verse one. In verse one, the Lord has already searched and known the psalmist. That is from the Lord's perspective and that is what the Lord has done. When we come to verse twenty-three, the psalmist invites the Lord to search him. He is willing: "Lord, you go right ahead and search me all around." The Lord already knows us, but if we want Him to be personal in our lives, we have to invite Him and be willing for Him to be in our lives. Note the earnestness in his prayer, "Search me, O God," and his aspiration for God to do so, "and know my heart." Jeremiah wrote:

> The heart is more deceitful than all else
> And is desperately sick;
> Who can understand it? (Je. 17:9)

You and I cannot know our own hearts. Who can tell what wickedness resides in our hearts? God knows. He knows every intricate detail of our lives. If we know our God better, we will know ourselves better and we will want Him to search our hearts and to try us: "Test me, Lord, and know my anxious thoughts. Lord, see if there be any hurtful way in me, because I don't know if it's there. And lead me in the everlasting way. Lord, I want to go with plan A and I want You to lead me. I cannot do it by myself, Lord. You already know me. Maybe I've resisted it before, but now I am totally open to it, and I invite you to come. Now from my perspective, Lord, I want You there." That is what the Lord is waiting for. That is the key that unlocks the door to being personal with God.

My Response

When we know God better, we will know ourselves better. Because God is intimately acquainted with us, we will be intimate with other people. When we really know that God is present in our lives, loneliness will depart from us and we will become sensitive to other lonely people. When we know that God has invested His power in making us, we will understand that we are of infinite worth to Him, and that other people are of infinite worth to Him as well. God's precious thoughts are toward us and they outnumber the sand. For God spent all that energy to make us who we are, it is not without a purpose. He has a plan. He is going to lead us in it, and He is going to protect us in it. Now it is up to us.

Are you willing? Will you invite the Lord? "Lord, go right ahead. I want to go your way, the everlasting way." It is the decision you and I have to make. How personal is your God? Do you have fears in your life? Do you find it difficult to relate to other people? Do you have a lot of hang-ups? Do you accept yourself? Do you have anxieties and worries? Where is your God? He is there. He is desirous to be personal in your life, but you have to invite Him. Can you do that?

The more we know God, the more we will know ourselves. The more we are intimate with God, the more we can be intimate with others. Jesus Christ has already died on the cross for our sins. He rose again from the dead. Why do you and I continue in sin? It is sin that keeps us away from God. He does not have to be far away. He is not far away. If He is far away, He has not moved. You and I need to invite Him back in. "Search me, O God, and know my heart." Are you willing to make that prayer to God? Are you willing to invite the Lord and yield your life to Him? Do you really want the Lord to search your heart?

HE WHO IS SPIRITUAL - PART I

One of the great truths the world has missed is that Man is a spiritual being. We know that Man is a physical being who does exercise for his body, Man is an intellectual being who goes to school to get an education, and Man is a social being who likes to be with people and learns to handle relationships with other people. We do not find any exercise, however, for the development of spirituality, because Man does not realize that he is a spiritual being.

Recently there have been studies concerning the spiritual world. They are more on the negative aspect, in areas such as extrasensory perception, psychic phenomenon, and demonology. Our God wants us to know that we are spiritual beings and that He has something wonderful for those who are spiritual.

Purpose of Divine Creation

One of the greatest tragedies in education today is the teaching that Man was evolved from animals and Man is only an animal. We know that we are not animals, because we know how God created Man. He created Man differently from animals. Let us review what Man is. Genesis 2:7 says:

> Then the LORD God formed man of dust from the ground, and breathed into his nostrils the breath of life; and man became a living being.

If you want to know how to make a man, the formula is right here. You take a little dust, you add "the breath of life," and you will get a living man. Scientists today have been trying to discover the truth about life. We need to tell them that it is right here in the Bible. We see God taking a personal interest in making Man. With the animals God just said:

> "Let the earth bring forth living creatures after their kind...."
> (Gn. 1:24)

But with Man, God took special care and breathed into him "the breath of life." This is the very life of God.

Another word we use to translate "the breath of life" is the word "spirit." When the "breath" or the "spirit" of a man goes away, the man dies, for he is no longer a living soul. But as long as a man has "the breath of life" or the "spirit," then he is a living soul. So, Man has a spirit, and he is a spiritual being.

Functions of Man's Spirit

What does the spirit do? If we study this word and find all other places in the Bible where it has been mentioned, we will be able to see the functions of the spirit.

44

The spiritual understanding   Job 32:8 says:

> But it is a spirit in man,
> And the breath of the Almighty gives them understanding.

Here, we have the word "breath" and the word "spirit." The word "breath" is the same word as in Genesis 2:7. In fact, you might want to write down Job 32:8 next to Genesis 2:7 for your own reference. When "the breath" comes to a man, it does something to him. According to Job 32:8, it gives him understanding. This is one of the functions of the spirit of Man. When God's breath comes into a man, he receives understanding. It is a spiritual understanding, not an intellectual understanding.

Take reading the Bible as an example. Anybody can read the Bible—it is just words in a book; that is all it is. Anybody can read the Bible, but not everyone can understand it, because to understand it a person needs spiritual understanding. Too many people try to understand the Bible with their intellect, and so they do not understand it with their spirit. But one of the functions of the spirit is to give us spiritual understanding.

The discerning conscience   Turn next to Proverbs 20:27. You might want to write this reference verse next to Genesis 2:7 as well.

> The spirit of man is the lamp of the LORD,
> Searching all the innermost parts of his being.

This word "spirit" is the same word as "breath" in Genesis 2:7. It is the "lamp of the LORD." A lamp lights up the dark areas, and it searches the innermost parts. The word "searching" does not mean trying to find answers to questions, but it means to penetrate the heart. It shows things, inside us, that we did not know before. It corrects the misunderstandings we have. It lights up the darkened areas. Because of "the breath of life," now we know things which we did not know before. It tells us what is right and what is wrong; what is true and what is false. At first, we might have thought that something was right, but when we have the lamp, then we know that it is wrong. We have a word for that "something" inside us that tells us what is right and what is wrong: the conscience. And that is another function of the spirit.

The problem with people today is that their spirit is dead. The Bible tells us that we were once dead in our trespasses and sins (Eph. 2:1). Of course, we are still biologically alive, but our spirit is dead. That is, it is not functioning properly. Every man has a spirit, but because of sin, the spirit is distorted. Every man has a sense that there is a God, but he cannot understand the true God. Every man has a conscience, a sense of right and wrong, but the conscience is distorted. What is right for you may be wrong for me; what was wrong yesterday may be right today. And so we do not know anymore. We may think that we know, but we really do not. This shows us that our spirit is distorted, it is dead and it is not functioning properly. Our spirit must become alive in order for it to function properly. Then, we will know how to make the right decisions, the decisions we make every moment of our lives.

The right decision   You had to make a decision this morning. When your alarm clock went off, you had to make a decision—either you turn off the alarm and get up, or you throw it out of the window and stay in bed. We make decisions every moment of our lives: "Should I brush my teeth now or wait until tomorrow?" "What am I going to buy when I go shopping?" "What shall I cook for dinner tonight?" "Shall I talk to this person or not?" "Shall I make that telephone call?" "What shall I do about my business?" "Shall I do my homework at school?"

Every moment of our lives, we have to make decisions.

But what is going to control those decisions? Every man has a will. You can do anything you want. Our will is very strong, but our will is controlled by certain factors. What if I want to tear my hair out and go screaming out the door? But I will not do it. Why will I not do it? It is because I will be embarrassed: "What will people think of me?"

Many of our decisions are controlled by what other people think or do. Sometimes we do certain things, because that is the way Chinese do things. Or, we do not do certain things, because Chinese do not do so. Our decisions are based upon cultural values. Some of us depend on the way we have been raised in our families. Some are shy: they do not talk to anybody; they just stay home and study. And some are extroverts: they love to talk; they go everywhere and they are very loud.

What you and I do in life today is based on external factors. When we make decisions, we see what other people think and we look at the worldly values. We have certain feelings. We do things because we feel like it. Our conscience cannot discern what is right and what is wrong, because it is often guided by what the society says. Everybody else is doing it, so I will do it too; since nobody is doing it, I am not going to do it. Nobody is preaching out there in the street and nobody is witnessing, so I am not going to witness. Our conscience does not know what is right or what is wrong anymore. Therefore, we make wrong decisions. We make decisions based on our intellect also. We think: "After all, I have been educated and I have a degree, so I can make decisions." Then we realize that we make so many wrong decisions, because we are not spiritual. To be spiritual should be the factor that controls our decision making. It is the basis of our decision making.

What we need is to know God's truth. When our

understanding opens up, we can understand His Word and the Holy Spirit will apply His Word in our hearts. And then we will know what is right and what is wrong, because God tells us. We will do things because God says so, not because what other people say. We need to be spiritual.

Consequences of Being Spiritual

Now what does it mean by "to be spiritual"? When we think about spiritual people, we have all kinds of thoughts. We think of ghosts; we think of disembodied spirits floating around. But that is not spiritual. That is being mystical. The Bible tells us what it means to be spiritual. We are going to see that to be spiritual is very practical and it is for our lives today.

Appraising all things   Let us take a look at 1 Corinthians 2:15:

> But he who is spiritual appraises all things . . . .

A spiritual person can appraise all things. This word "appraise" means to "have judgment, discernment." In real estate, there are appraisers who determine the value of property. The idea of this word is to take a shifter full of sand and you shift, shift and shift and then you get the gold out of that shifter of sand. So "to be able to determine value" is the idea of this word. A spiritual person can appraise, not some things, not one thing, but all things.

Maybe you had a tragedy in your family or some terrible things happened. If you are spiritual, you will know that God will take care of you. Even though emotionally it is very difficult, yet when you appraise the situation, you know that God is going to work everything together for good to those who love Him (Rom. 8:28). It does not look like it, but you trust God and you can appraise it. Maybe, in school, your professor says that evolution is true. He is the professor, but because you are spiritual, you can appraise what he says. You can tell the professor, "Professor, you are wrong, for the Bible said that it is not true." You start with the Bible, so your presuppositions are from the Bible. But your professor's presuppositions are from himself. Our authority comes from God; the professor's authority comes from men.

We have a higher authority. We can evaluate and appraise whatever our education teaches us. For example, we can appraise whether the history books are right or not. There is a civilization called the "Hittites" in the Bible. The scholars used to laugh and scoff at the Bible, because there was no such people. Then in 1920, they dug up a civilization called...guess what? The "Hittites." The Bible is accurate and is true. Because we have the Bible, we can be spiritual. Maybe, at work, your boss tells you to do something. You can determine whether it is right or not. If you have a relationship problem, you can appraise the situation. Because you have the Bible and you are spiritual, you know what you must do to straighten out that relationship.

Appraised by no man It also says in 1 Corinthians 2:15:

> he himself is appraised by no man.

If you are spiritual, people will not understand you. They cannot figure you out. Why do you talk about Jesus so much? Why do you go to church so often? Why do you not stay home on Wednesday nights instead of going to prayer meetings? No man can understand you, because you are spiritual. No man can appraise or evaluate your life. If you are spiritual, you will receive criticism and you will have persecution. But that is all right, because you expect it. Even Jesus Christ, the most spiritual person, was criticized.

Away from the fleshly In 1 Corinthians 3:1, Paul said to the Corinthians that he could not speak to them as spiritual men, but as immature babes in Christ, as men of flesh. Here were some people who were not spiritual. In verse two, Paul told them that he could not give them solid food, but milk. A person who is not spiritual cannot really understand the Bible; he is too fleshly. It says in verse three that there was jealousy and strife in their midst. They were having problems in their relationships. They were full of petty jealousy, anger and bitterness in relationships. And because of that, it prevented them from being spiritual. That tells us we need to get rid of those things. It is not worthwhile to remain angry at someone, especially our own brother or sister in Christ. It will prevent us from being spiritual; we will be full of burdens and bound by chains. We will be torturing ourselves.

God has a plan for this world. God is moving in a direction. The Kingdom of God is coming! But we are so wound up in our own little problems, strifes and petty jealousies that we cannot see, with the eyes of God, the total picture of what He is doing in this world. Let us get rid of that strife and jealousy. Let us be spiritual, because that is freedom, that is power and that is living! Although we are Christians, some of us have all kinds of relationship problems. When those things are gone, there is such freedom: the chains are unshackled. You have freedom and power in Christ if you are spiritual: no more strife, no more anger, no more bitterness and no more jealousy.

Trusting the Bible Let us look at another verse, 1 Corinthians 14:37:

> If anyone thinks he is a prophet or spiritual, let him recognize that the things which I write to you are the Lord's commandment.

Paul wrote to the Corinthians; you know that it was not just Paul—it was God Himself. Yes, men did write the Bible, but

God superintended and God controlled the whole thing. The Bible is, in fact, the Lord's commandments to us. If you are not spiritual, you say, "Oh, the Bible has contradictions. The Bible is full of errors." But if you are spiritual, you trust the Bible, you know the Bible and you love the Bible.

I cannot understand some people who say "Well, I read the Bible, but I don't get anything out of it." I say, "You don't get anything out of the Bible?! Do you know what this Bible is? This Bible is the very Word of God—it is God Himself speaking! It is a record of the mighty acts of God! When you read it, you get nothing out of it?!" I tell you, if you want to talk about miracles, the Bible is a miracle! If you are not spiritual, of course the Bible seems dead. But if you are spiritual, you would rather read the Bible than the newspaper, because the Bible is alive and is exciting. That comes only when you are spiritual.

Caring for others   Galatians 6:1 says:

> Brethren, even if a man is caught in any trespass, you who are spiritual, restore such a one in a spirit of gentleness; each one looking to yourself, lest you too be tempted.

Here is a spiritual person who will have a ministry with people. He will care about the spiritual well-being of another person. If he knows that someone is having problems or someone has been overcome by sin, he will want to help this person, not out of pride, but with a spirit of gentleness. He will love the person. If you are truly spiritual, you have love, you care for people and you want to help those who are down.

Some of the most spiritual men in our church are our deacons. We have early morning prayer meetings at 6:30 am. Our deacons care for you. We do not just talk about you; we pray for you and plan how we can help you. We are for you and we love you. Let us all do that. If all of you men become deacons and all of you women become deacons' wives, that will be terrific! Let us be spiritual.

Be Spiritual

The blessed way I want to be spiritual. If I am spiritual, I can appraise all things. If I am spiritual, nobody can really criticize me, because they cannot understand. If I am spiritual, I know that the Bible is God's Word. If I am spiritual, I can get rid of all my strifes and jealousies. If I am spiritual, I am in the business of helping people. That is freedom, that is power and that is real living!

A spiritual person will live and make decisions according to the Word of God. That is why Jesus died on the Cross, and that is why Jesus came. 1 John 5:20 says that Jesus:

> has come, and has given us understanding . . . .

When Jesus comes into our heart to take away our sins, we can understand God. Every person has the capacity and the potential to understand the things of God. When we know the things of God, our conscience is shaped up the right way and we will really know what is right and what is wrong. The Spirit of God will apply the principles of God's Word in our hearts, then we can make the proper decisions. We can know what to do. After that it becomes a matter of whether or not we will obey God.

The hard way But so many people are not spiritual. They are merely psychological and fleshly. They make their decisions according to their own thinking, their own feelings, or what other people say or do. Their will is determined by society, rather than by God's truth. Some of you are faced with a major decision right now. Society has told you what to do, and you want to follow what society dictates. You have mixed feelings perhaps. You are thinking all kinds of different ways. Maybe you are thinking selfishly of yourself, and you are going to take the easy way out. Well, in reality it is the hard way, because you are not listening to the voice of God.

If God tells you what is true, trust God and be spiritual, regardless of your feelings. Even if you think that you cannot handle it, trust God and follow God's way. God will take care of you. People may tell you to do things this way, but listen to God. No one can understand why you are doing things that way, because a spiritual person is appraised by no man. Be spiritual, so that you will be free to live God's way.

Brothers and sisters, God is moving in a direction. He is inviting you and me to join Him, but He can only take the spiritual ones. Many of us are not spiritual. Our will is not shaped according to God's will, but is controlled by wrong factors. Therefore, we make the wrong decisions and we are not going God's way. Let us be spiritual.

The obedient way   Next time, I will go into more detail about how to be spiritual. For now, what I have shared is just an introduction to making proper decisions by listening to the Spirit of God. But I have shared something practical. Some of you are still having relationship problems. You need to straighten them out.

So many of you are dependent upon your emotions. For example somebody gets angry at you and yells at you, "You did this!" Your natural reaction is to yell back, "Oh, no! I didn't! You did it!" Then he yells louder, "No, you did it!!" You climb up the mountain and you say, "No, you did it!!!" You get nowhere that way. If you know God's truth and if the Spirit of God applies it in your heart, you will make the right decision and do the right thing. To all those times you are

53

making emotional decisions to yell back, what does God's Word say? Proverbs 15:1 says:

> A gentle answer turns away wrath,
> But a harsh word stirs up anger.

When you study that verse, you understand that a soft answer turns away wrath and that is the way to handle it. Your conscience tells you: It is right to give a gentle answer; it is wrong to shout harsh words to stir up more anger. The Holy Spirit works in your heart, and the Spirit of God tests you. He allows you to get into an argument with someone. That person yells at you, and you are ready to yell back at him. Emotions start rising and by your feelings you are about to make a decision to yell back at him. But you have read Proverbs 15:1 and the Holy Spirit works in your heart. With that soft, soft prompting, He says, "Gentle answer, gentle answer." Now are you going to be controlled by your emotions or by the Spirit of God? Suppose he yells at you, and you say, "Well, that's very interesting. Why don't you tell me a little bit more?" "Why did you do this and that?" "Oh, I don't know. I'm not sure. Can you say it again please?" And you find that the emotions will die down, because you are in control. In reality, it is the Holy Spirit that is in control. Because you are spiritual, you will not let your emotions guide you.

We are not perfect. Sometimes we do get emotional. We are emotional beings, we are intellectual beings and we are social beings. But brothers and sisters, let us not forget that we are spiritual beings as well! There is a power many of us have not experienced yet. I want so much for you to experience that power, so that everyone of you can be spiritual. I know that it is true and it can work in your lives. Some of you have experienced it already. Praise the Lord! It is only by God's grace we shall all be spiritual.

HE WHO IS SPIRITUAL - PART II

Obstacles to Spirituality

One fundamental truth the world has missed is that Man is a spiritual being. Of course, he is a physical being and a social being, but he is a spiritual being as well. The Bible tells us that God breathed His Spirit into Man, and this "breath of life" is what made Man alive. We have also discovered the two functions of that Spirit. One function is spiritual understanding: Because Man has a spirit, he can understand the things of God. The other function is that of his conscience: Man can know what is right and what is wrong. So, Man has spiritual understanding and Man has a conscience.

A spiritual death But sin came in. Because of sin also came death—spiritual death. The Bible says that we were dead in our trespasses and sins (Eph. 2:1). We do not have a relationship with God as we ought to have. Our spiritual understanding is darkened, so we cannot understand the things of God. And our conscience is defiled such that we no longer know what is right and what is wrong. Things become relative. That which used to be wrong is right today; that which is right for you is wrong for me.

Man still has a spirit, but because of sin, it is not functioning properly. It is distorted. All over the world, men worship "god," but the wrong one. Man still has a conscience but it is distorted as well. The Bible tells us in Titus 1:15:

> To the pure, all things are pure; but to those who are defiled and unbelieving, nothing is pure, but both their mind and their conscience are defiled.

The unbelieving mind and the conscience are defiled, filthy and distorted. Because of sin, Man cannot know the things of God, and Man does not know right from wrong. That is why Jesus Christ came. Please turn to 1 John 5:20:

> And we know that the Son of God has come, and has given us understanding, in order that we might know Him who is true, and we are in Him who is true, in His Son Jesus Christ. This is the true God and eternal life.

Jesus came to restore to us our proper spiritual understanding. If we truly receive Jesus into our heart, our understanding is opened. Then we can understand the things of God. We have the potential; we can learn and we can really know God.

A spiritual relationship   When God created Adam, He had a spiritual relationship with Adam, because God is spirit. The Bible talks about how God talked to Adam and how Adam talked to God. It was a spiritual relationship. Later, Eve was tempted in the garden. The serpent made her use her intellect to rationalize and to argue, so she tried to explain and argue with Satan. (If you and I use only our mind, trying to think and argue with Satan, we will fail.) Then, Eve saw that the tree was good for food. Her emotions were stirred up. By her intellectual reasoning and by her emotions, she took the fruit and ate it. That was how she made her decision. She made it based on her rationale and her emotions—and she made the wrong decision.

When Adam and Eve knew that they were naked, they had shame and guilt. They were always naked, but all of a sudden it meant something, because their conscience was affected. They knew that it was wrong, so they sewed fig leaves to cover themselves and hid in the bushes from the presence of the Lord. God was seeking them out, but they were hiding in the bushes. The understanding and relationship with God was cut off. That is how it is with you and me today. Some of us sense that God is so far away. But, He is not! He is ever so close. We are the ones who are hiding; God is the one who is seeking. We have got to come out of the bushes, repent and confess our sins. Then, we will be able to restore that spiritual relationship with God.

Objectives of Spirituality

Why is it so important to be spiritual? It all comes down to the matter of decision making. You and I make decisions every moment of our lives. Some of us have to make major decisions; some, minor. It is important what kind of decision you and I will make. What is going to control and direct your decision making? Would it be your own "self"? "I do what I like. I'll do it if I feel like it. I do it because other people are doing it." Or, are you doing it because God is in control? It is very important for us to have a spiritual relationship with God.

A spiritual battle I would like you to look at another verse, Ephesians 6:12:

> For our struggle is not against flesh and blood, but against the rulers, against the powers, against the world forces of this darkness, against the spiritual forces of wickedness in the heavenly places.

Our struggle is not with flesh and blood, but with the powers of Satan. That argument with your husband or with your wife is not only flesh and blood. The problems and temptations in your job and in your family are not just flesh and blood. There is a spiritual element to that fight, to that argument and to that bitterness. Because you and I are not as spiritual as we ought to be, we fail to realize that the real battle is a spiritual battle. We are trying to fight it on the flesh and blood front, but the real battle is on the frontlines with spiritual forces. The only way we can fight this battle is with spiritual weapons. But we work with flesh and blood. We argue with people; we have conflicts with people; we are bitter, we envy and we hold grudges. We do not realize that this spiritual battle is a matter of sin in our lives, nor do we realize that it is on the spiritual level. It is because we are not spiritual. Once we become spiritual, we are going to see that, "Yes, that's where the real conflict is." So, it is important for us to be spiritual, because the real battle is a spiritual one.

A spiritual Kingdom   In   Matthew 7:21, Jesus says:

> Not every one who says to Me, "Lord, Lord," will enter the
> kingdom of heaven; but he who does the will of My Father
> who is in heaven.

There it is. It is a matter of the right decision. Are you doing the will of God? You will never do the will of God unless you are spiritual. What does God want to do? He wants to work in your life. He has a Kingdom and He is inviting you and me to enter into His Kingdom. But we will never enter into His Kingdom unless we are doing His will, and we will never do His will unless we are spiritual.

A spiritual obedience   Jesus Christ was a man. He was a true man. Let us look at Matthew chapter twenty-six. This is where Jesus was in the Garden of Gethsemane. He went there to pray. In verse thirty-seven it says:

> He took with Him Peter and the two sons of Zebedee, and
> began to be grieved and distressed.

We see the tremendous emotions of our Lord. Because He was so distressed He needed people around Him. When you and I are distressed, we need people around us. In verse thirty-eight, He told them how His soul was deeply grieved to the point of death. He needed His brothers to pray with Him and pray for Him. Such tremendous emotions and such terrific pressure were pressing against our Lord! He was on the threshold of being nailed to the cross. In verse thirty-nine, He prayed that famous prayer:

> not as I will, but as Thou wilt.

In spite of tremendous emotions, our Lord Jesus made the right choice according to the Spirit of God. He was perfectly spiritual. He did the will of God, although His emotions were telling Him otherwise. He reproved and warned his disciples:

> "Keep watching and praying, . . .the spirit is willing, but
> the flesh is weak." (Mt. 26:41)

That is so true. Most of us here do have a willing spirit— we want to do the will of God, we want to read the Bible, we want to pray and we want to go to church. The spirit is willing, but the flesh is weak. It is not enough to have a willing spirit. We must also have a strong spirit. We must have an obedient spirit. What we so desire according to the Spirit of God, we will also do.

Options of Spirituality

A spiritual man The Bible tells us that there are three kinds of people. Let us look at 1 Corinthians 2:15:

> But he who is spiritual appraises all things, yet he himself
> is appraised by no man.

This is a spiritual person. That is what we want to be: A spiritual person who appraises all things. No matter what the situation is and no matter what the relationship problem is, he can estimate the value and he knows the "what-to-do." To be a spiritual person is practical. It is not something way up in the air we can never achieve. It is something down to earth you and I can do. When we are spiritual, we can do things. Why is this person spiritual? He has received "not the spirit of the world, but the Spirit who is from God" (1 Cor. 2:12). A spiritual person receives the Spirit who is from God. If you have truly received the Spirit who is from God, you can know the things freely given to you by God.

But I am afraid that many Christians are more receptive to the spirit who is from the world. We remember that when the Spirit of God entered into Man, it made Man alive. The Spirit of God is a source of life: It animated the body and made it living. The spirit of the world does that also. The spirit of the world is that which makes the world come alive. If we have the Spirit who is from God, God will never become boring but will always be exciting.

A natural man The second kind of man is found in 1 Corinthians 2:14:

> a natural man does not accept the things of the Spirit of
> God; for they are foolishness to him, and he cannot
> understand them, because they are spiritually appraised.

A natural man cannot accept the things of God. He cannot even understand them. "Foolishness! Jesus rose from the dead!" "Foolishness! What do you go to church for?" "Why do you go to prayer meeting? Foolishness!" "Stay home to watch television. That's better." The natural man cannot understand spiritual things. The word "natural" in the original language actually means a "soulish man," one who is only of the soul. A natural man is an unbeliever. All he has is his own self. Whatever decision he makes is based upon himself: What he thinks and what he feels. Therefore, his authority is himself. "Why do you think that way?" "Because I think that way." "Why do you do that?" "Because I feel like it." "I am the authority"—that is a natural man. But when you become a Christian, you do not have to be a natural man, because now you have a new nature and you have the Spirit of God. You can be spiritual. You do not need to listen to yourself. You have a higher authority now. When Jesus saves you, He saves you from your "self." Your "self" is limited, but the Spirit of God is unlimited.

A fleshly man The third kind of man is in 1 Corinthians chapter three. It talks about the fleshly man in verse two:

> I gave you milk to drink, not solid food; for you were not yet able to receive it. Indeed, even now you are not yet able. . . .

These were not new Christians. We are not talking about new converts; we are talking about people who had been Christians for a while. Many of us have been Christians for a long time. Are we still fleshly? It says in 1 Corinthians 3:3:

> for you are still fleshly. For since there is jealousy and strife among you, are you not fleshly, and are you not walking like mere men?

These were Christians who refused to grow. They went back to their old selfish ways. Jesus delivered them from themselves and they had free access to the Spirit of God, but they went back to their "selves." They were fleshly with jealousy and strife; they had a lot of pride; and they walked like mere men, the natural men. Although they were Christians, they still looked like non-Christians. Brothers and sisters, God has called us to be spiritual. Let us come out of our fleshliness.

Opportunities for Spirituality

How are we going to be spiritual? I can only share one thing with you today. It is the enlightenment God has given here, which you and I have to get hold of.

A spiritual differentiation In order for us to be spiritual, we must differentiate between our soul and our spirit. That is pretty hard to do, because the soul and the spirit are so intertwined with each other. So, when we do things, we have to ask ourselves, "Is it coming from our soul? Or, is it coming from our spirit?" How do we know we are making the right decision? We will never know unless we know the difference between our soul and our spirit. If we do not know the difference, we will have an inconsistent life—sometimes operating according to the soul and sometimes according to the spirit.

A spiritual devotion

a. Functions of the Word of God Hebrews 4:12 says:

> For the word of God is living and active and sharper than any two-edged sword, and piercing as far as the division of soul and spirit, of both joints and marrow, and able to judge the thoughts and intentions of the heart.

To divide soul and spirit, we need the Word of God. If we are not into God's Word, we will never be able to know the division between soul and spirit. You and I are not only to know the Word of God but also to experience the Word of

God. The only way we can experience it is by really getting into it.

There are four adjectives given to the Word of God here. It is living, it is active, it is sharp and it is piercing. The Word of God is living: it has life and it can give life. You and I are born again by the Word of God which lives and abides forever. The Word of God is active: it is powerful and always accomplishes whatever God wants it to do. The Word of God can do things in your life and in my life. The Word of God is sharp and it is sharper than any two-edged sword. Not only does it cut but also pierces. The word "to pierce" is "to penetrate." That means it can go even deeper than a cut. This is how you can keenly divide between soul and spirit.

b. Studying the Word of God You must get into the Word of God to be spiritual. There is no substitute, and there is no short cut. You have to study it. You cannot say that you are in the Word of God, if you just read a few verses a day and read a devotional commentary after reading the few verses. You have to have long sittings to read the Word of God. Not only read the Word of God but also study the Word of God. You need to get a notebook, and write down what you learn about the Word of God. Write down the questions you do not understand. That is one of the most important things in Bible study—write down what you do not know. That will make you study further. When you study the Bible, very often you encounter things you do not know and you just forget them afterwards. You need a notebook. Besides that, you need to attend Church Training Program to learn how to study the Bible; you need to go to a Christian bookstore to read up on how to study the Bible; and you need to ask questions and talk to pastors, deacons and Sunday School teachers. You need to read the Bible everyday. I was challenged by a professor years ago. He said:

"Take the book of Philippians and read all four chapters. The first day, you just read the whole book, all four chapters, in one sitting. That is all. The second day, open to Philippians and read four chapters. That is it. The third day, read Philippians again. For thirty days, you read Philippians once a day in one sitting. Two things will happen at the end of the month. First, your Bible will be automatically opened to Philippians. Second, you will know Philippians."

What a challenge to do that with every book of the Bible! You say, "What do I do when I come to Genesis? I can't read that in one sitting." Here is where you divide the chapters. Maybe take just ten chapters of Genesis a day for one month or seven chapters of Matthew for one month. Maybe you want to do it in fifteen days. You decide, but read it. Not only read it but also study it. Go to Church Training Program to learn the methods to study the Bible. There is no short cut and there is no substitute. Without the Word of God penetrating your heart, you will never have a division into soul and spirit. And if that never happens, you will never know what it means to be spiritual. You must read the Bible. You must learn how to study the Bible. And you must read the Bible in long sittings.

c. Effects of the Word of God I met a young man in New York. He really learned the Bible. After the retreat, he went home. His parents yelled at him and got angry at him. This young man, for the first time, did not yell back. He was able to appraise the situation. He knew that his parents were yelling at him according to their emotions. After they finished, he did not talk back. He went to his room, knelt down and prayed. Although his emotions were there and he was angry, he was spiritually controlled. He prayed and he asked other people to pray for him. That was the first time he ever did that. He knew the difference between his soul and his spirit, because he was into studying the Word of God with me. The Word of God pierced his heart and divided between his soul and his spirit.

d. ***Starvation from the Word of God***   You and I cannot differentiate the soul from the spirit, unless we get into the Word of God. It is not going to work if you just come to hear the Word of God on Sundays. It is not going to work. Suppose you do not eat food for the whole week from Monday through Saturday and then on Sunday you have turkey, roast beef and all kinds of food. You will be sick and will not be able to eat. Your stomach has shrunk, because you have not eaten for the whole week. Many of us do not read the Bible for the whole week. We are spiritually starving when we come to Sunday. No wonder it is so hard for some of us to listen to preaching, or to sit in Sunday School. We cannot take it in, because we have been spiritually starved the whole week.

Get into the Bible. Do it the whole week and watch what happens. Your life will be changed. You will see a difference between your spirit and your soul, and you will be more spiritual.

WHEN I CRY, GOD IS SILENT

There comes a time in every person's life when he has to take off the mask and cry out from the anguish of his soul. There are many of you who have different kinds of burdens in your life, but it seems like heaven does not move to alleviate those deep burdens. Perhaps you can identify with some of the psalmists in the book of Psalms:

> Why dost Thou stand afar off, O LORD?
> Why dost Thou hide Thyself in times of trouble? (Ps.
>   10:1)

> How long shall I take counsel in my soul,
> Having sorrow in my heart all the day?
> How long will my enemy be exalted over me? (Ps.
>   13:2)

> My God, my God, why hast Thou forsaken me?
> Far from my deliverance are the words of my groaning.
>   (Ps. 22:1)

There are many, many other psalms like these. And maybe in

the midst of your troubles you cry out like that. . .but God does not seem to answer.

How do you answer a man who wants to live but has an incurable disease? What do you say to a child who questions God about why He allowed a fatal accident to take away the life of his/her mother? Or, how do you respond to a young girl who does not feel any love and does not feel like she belongs, even in the church? We cry out to God with our hearts. . . and there is nothing but silence.

There were two sisters in the Bible whose brother had died. They sent a message to Jesus calling for His help. Jesus was their friend, and He had spent a lot of time together with these two sisters, Mary and Martha, and their brother Lazarus. Jesus was the one who could miraculously cure the sick. People would approach Him as He was walking along the road—even perfect strangers—and He would heal them. How much more, certainly, Jesus would come and help His friends! But their brother had died. These two sisters were grief stricken, almost as if to say, "Jesus, you failed me! I'm disappointed! This disproves that You are the Son of God!"

The Reason for God's Silence

When their brother Lazarus was sick, these sisters sent a message to Jesus, "Lord, behold, he whom You love is sick" (John 11:3). In verse four, it says, "Jesus heard it." And Jesus hears you. There is never a cry the Lord does not hear. Any prayer from a sincere heart, the Lord hears. Then verse four continues with the Lord's response:

"This sickness is not unto death, but for the glory of God...."

When we think of death, we think of it as the worst possible consequence. Here, we are to take comfort to know that whatever we are going through, it will never, never be the worst possible consequence! If we truly are the children of God, He will care for us. Whatever happens, it will be for the glory of God.

Magnificent in purpose So Lazarus did die, but it was only momentary—it was not for eternity. One day, Lazarus, after he was raised from the dead, would die again. You and I cry for healing for our sickness. Even if we are healed, we will get sick again. We cry for deliverance from our troubles. After we are delivered, trouble from somewhere else will come again. This is the reality of life. Have you ever had a loved one who died? If you have not, you will. At that time, we cry out to God and there is silence. The first principle we need to recognize is: It will be for the glory of God. It is not for our own selfish gain. Our whole lives are to be for the glory of God.

Jesus could have come and healed Lazarus. If He had healed him from his sickness, it would have been tremendous. But Jesus came and raised him from the dead. It was not only tremendous but also glorious! Our God is not in the business of accommodating Himself to our whims and ways of wanting to see certain answers. God's ways are higher than our ways; His thoughts are higher than our thoughts. We may look at our problem, analyze the situation, and then think that the only way to solve our problem is this particular way. But oftentimes God will answer in His way, so that He will be glorified and we will know that that is His way.

There is a brother in our church. I telephoned him and asked him if I could have permission to share this illustration of his life, and he said that I could. This brother has been having a lot of problems. There were physical problems in his family, and there were financial problems. In spite of all these problems, this past Thanksgiving he came to the church service and thanked God. Do you know what happened after that testimony? His car was stolen that very night. Here, he was giving testimony to God's glory; there, his car was stolen. It was a hard lesson to learn. Later, the police found the car. It was abandoned and stripped. Everything had been taken. He was bewildered, "What's happening?" But praise be to God. The insurance company gave him more money than he expected. When everything was settled, he was able to buy another car that was better than the one he had, and he had money left over to pay all his bills, plus extra money besides that. May glory be to God! God works in His way! Sometimes we cry out and there is silence; but it just means that God is working it out His way.

Supreme in love In John 11:5, it says:

> Now Jesus loved Martha, and her sister, and Lazarus.

The Lord loved them, and He loves you. This word "love" is where we get the word "agape love." This is the sacrificial love. This is the love that has purpose and direction. This is the deep love the Lord has. In verse three, they sent the message saying:

> "Lord, behold, he whom You love is sick."

This word "love" is a different Greek word. This word <u>phileo</u> φιλέω means affectionate love, emotional love. There is nothing wrong with that kind of love, and the Lord does love us like that. But, note the difference between these loves. From the human perspective, the sisters tried to describe the kind of love the Lord had for Lazarus. They thought that His love was a brotherly love, an affectionate love. But actually, the Lord Himself has a deeper love than that. We cry out to the Lord, "Lord, you're supposed to love me! Why do you allow these things to happen?" We have the wrong concept of His love. God does love us, but it is a deeper love than you or I can ever imagine.

Look at the love He had. What did He do? It says in verse six:

> When therefore He heard that he was sick, He stayed then two days longer. . . .

Because He loves, He deliberately stayed back two days. He left Lazarus to die! Sometimes you and I cry out to the Lord...but He is silent. He does not seem to answer us. We should realize that. He deliberately does not answer us because He has a purpose. He loves us and His love is great! When we are hurt, our God hears us. He is not playing games with us—He is not a foolish God; He is not being cruel—He is not a cruel God; and He is not unaware of what is happening—He is not an ignorant God. We know all these things; but we are human, and when these things happen we still feel the pain.

The Reaction to God's Silence

After Lazarus died, we see the reactions of Mary and Martha and the range of emotions they had. Martha was the one who said to Him in John 11:21:

> Lord, if You had been here, my brother would not have died.

There is almost a hint of anger. Then when Mary came to the Lord, she said the same thing and she was crying.

Overwhelming emotions How did Jesus respond to them? We never find the Lord rebuking the sisters for their emotions. He did not say to them, "Why are you crying? I thought that you believed I'm the Son of God. What are you crying about? You should know better!" You never find the

Lord with that kind of attitude. He is understanding and very sympathetic. It says in John 11:35:

> Jesus wept.

That is very very profound, probably one of the most profound verses in the Bible. Jesus, who is the Son of God, the Christ, the God of all, the King of kings and Lord of lords, the Creator of the universe, the Almighty God Himself, the One who is holy and pure, the One who is completely separate from His creation, the One who causes fear in the hearts of men, and the One who will judge those who will not believe in Him, wept.

Do you know what this tells us? It is all right to feel and to have emotions. The Lord knows our hearts and pains. He identifies with our sufferings. The Lord knows what we are going through. He has even called the whole body of Christ, the Church, to rejoice and weep together. We need a little bit more crying in this church. Oh, I do not mean a forced display of emotions but a natural and spontaneous expression of emotions. When we see hurt, we need to express it. If we hide it, we are putting on a mask. Then people do not know what is really going on inside us. It is all right to cry, and it is all right for a man to cry. Jesus was the perfect man and Jesus wept. He understands our situations.

Theoretical rationalization Not only is there an emotional reaction, but also another reaction that happens when we are in pain. In response to Jesus' saying, "Your brother shall rise again" (Jn. 11:23), Martha said in verse twenty-four:

> "I know that he will rise again in the resurrection on the last day."

In the Greek language, there are several words that can be used for "I know." In this case, Martha was saying, "I fully know; I know it all." You and I know a lot of things. We have all the pat answers. We have all the theoretical knowledge.

Martha was thinking, "I know that, but what good is that? My brother is dead now! I know that he will be raised on the last day!" But Jesus confronted her and said, "I am the resurrection." You see, what she knew was true. Yes, there will be a resurrection, but do you know what Jesus was saying? He was saying, "Yes, the last day, and THIS is the last day." That is what the Bible says to you and to me. We are now living in the last day. Jesus has come and the resurrection is here! He is the resurrection and He is the life. If you believe in Him, you will never die. Even if you were to die, you would live again. And so the Lord confronted Martha with her theoretical knowledge.

You and I have a lot of theoretical knowledge. When trouble, pain and suffering come into our lives, we cry to God, but there is silence. What this knowledge does is to prepare the way for a new enlightenment. The agony and the pain you and I suffer are plowing the ground and fertilizing the soil for the abundant fruit to come. You can be well assured that there will come a day when the Lord will break the silence.

The Revelation after God's Silence

Finally, after two days of waiting, the Lord said, "Now it's time to go." In John 11:8, His disciples tried to stop Him. "You can't go back there. They're going to stone you!" But nothing would deter the Lord from going. And you can be sure that if it is time for the Lord to break the silence in your life, He will come and nothing will stop Him.

A new truth Maybe some of you have been looking for God, but you cannot find Him. There has been silence between you and God. Perhaps you do not even care about God. You are just living your own life and do not think too much about God. You had better wake up! When the Lord is ready to come, He will come and nothing will stop Him. He will break the silence. When He comes, He will confront you with the real truth. No longer will there be theoretical knowledge, nor the pat answers. So today, if you are crying out to God with the sincerity of your heart and God does not seem to answer, and you really do not sense that there is any particular sin in your life, you should know that God loves you. What God is going to do will be for His glory, and He will break the silence one day. He is going to show you some new truth, and there will be a challenge to your faith.

A greater challenge You see, the Lord made this great statement:

> "I am the resurrection and the life. . . ." (Jn. 11:25)

At the end of verse twenty-six, He asks, "Do you believe this?" It is a movement from knowledge to faith! You can be sure that when God breaks the silence, there is going to be a challenge to your faith.

Martha, in verse twenty-seven, made her great confession. She said, "Yes, Lord; I have believed that You are the Christ." The tense of the verb she used shows that she believed it in the past, she is believing it in the present and she will believe it in the future. Do you have a faith like that? I know that now you believe, but can you also believe in the midst of pain and misery? By God's grace, are you determined to believe, even in the future? That is the challenge God will give you. You need to believe. If you do not believe, you are lost.

Are you crying out to God? He does not seem to be close in your life; you still have trouble and problems. Wait upon the Lord. He is withholding from you for now, but because He loves you, He will answer you beyond your imagination. He will do it His way so that He will be glorified. When He is glorified, you will be happy. May God help us to trust in Him.

It is all right to express your feelings. If you are angry, tell the Lord. If you are going to cry, cry before the Lord. You can talk to others as well. But remember, one day God will break the silence and He will turn around your theoretical knowledge. He will probe deeply into your understanding, and He will challenge your faith. Wait upon the Lord. The Lord knows your hurts. The Lord weeps with you. He loves you very much. But because He loves you and because He will be glorified, He may purposely delay. I encourage you to keep your prayers and keep reading God's Word. Even in times of silence, write down your thoughts. Tell God your thoughts. Seek counsel with godly men and godly women to help you, for God has called us to weep together.

GOD'S GRACE TO DO GOD'S WILL

How do you like the weather outside? When I woke up, it reminded me so much of my home in San Francisco. I hope that you did not wake up and say, "Oh, no! It's raining! I don't want to come out of the house." It is the Lord's day, and you want to come and worship Him. What a joy and what a pleasure it is to be able to look into God's Word.

The Importance of God's Will

Some may not enter His Kingdom Let us look into God's Word about the Kingdom in Matthew 7:21:

> Not everyone who says to Me, "Lord, Lord," will enter the kingdom of heaven; but he who does the will of My Father who is in heaven.

This is a very serious verse. It is not enough to know that He is the Lord. It is not enough to know His name and be able to call on His name. It is not even enough to do a lot of good deeds. We see all the good deeds some did in verse twenty-two. They were even able to cast out demons and perform miracles, but the Lord said to them, "I never knew you." These were the ones who practiced lawlessness. They might have thought that they were doing good things in the name of the Lord, but the Lord said, "I never knew you." The word "to know" in the original has many meanings. It can mean "to have regard for" or "to recognize." If we add that in here, the Lord's reply will be "I never recognized you; I never had regard for what you did." They were practicing lawlessness. They were not practicing the standard of God. It is not enough to know the Lord, and it is not enough to do things in His name.

Those who do His will can It is only the one who does the will of his heavenly Father will enter the Kingdom of God. If you and I were to enter the Kingdom of heaven, it is because we do the will of God. In Matthew 7:24 we see a very famous illustration:

> Therefore everyone who hears these words of Mine, and acts upon them, may be compared to a wise man, who built his house upon the rock.

This wise man not only heard the Word but also acted upon it. On the contrary, the foolish man in verse twenty-six built his house upon the sand. He was the one who heard the Word of God but did not act upon it. So it is not enough to hear the Word of God, and it is not enough to know the Word of God. We have read the Bible and we have heard sermons, but it is no good unless we act upon the Word of God. If all we do is come here Sunday after Sunday to hear the sermon, and if that is all we do, then we are building our house on sand. We must act upon it, and we must do the will of God.

Knowing God's Will

God's will unfolding   "What is the will of God?"
Many of us have a misunderstanding of what the will of God
is. The will of God is not a giant blueprint or a map that is
dumped upon us, and then we know the will of God for the
rest of our lives. No! We may think of the will of God as a
scroll that slowly unfolds. It really is a daily, moment by
moment affair. We know the will of God day by day. God's
will is not a mystery, and it is not a foggy idea. God is more
than willing to show us His will. That is why He gave us
salvation, He gave us the Bible, He gave us prayer, He gave
us His Holy Spirit, He gave us the Church and He gave us
teachers and preachers. God wants to show His will to us. It
is not difficult to know the will of God. What needs to be
done is to do the will of God. You already know many things
that are the will of God. But the question is: Are you acting
upon what you already know?

When we go shopping in the store, many of us do what
we call "window-shopping." We go around looking at clothes
and store items, but we never buy anything. It is a good way
to save money. You see the nice clothes. Oh, you. . .you like
it. This is very nice. You try it on perhaps, but you never buy
it. You see all the nice appliances and the things you would
like to have, but you never possess them. There are many
Christians who are "window-shopping" Christians. They hear
the Word of God, they read the Bible, they see very nice things
in Christians' lives and they are very attracted to them.
Though they know all these qualities, yet the "window-
shopping" Christians never possess them. They have never
moved from knowing the will of God to actually doing the will
of God.

God's will executing   You already know some of God's will in the Bible. You know that you ought to go to church and you ought to worship God. But have you truly worshipped Him today? See, you know the will of God, but have you acted upon what you already know? You know that it is God's will to dedicate your life to Him and to put Jesus Christ first in your life. But, have you acted upon it? Is the Lord really first in your life? Are you really living a dedicated life? You know that you ought to pray. But, have you done it? You will be surprised that a lot of things you already know are the will of God.

Doing God's Will

How do we move from knowing God's will to doing God's will? There is a gap in between. We need something to bridge the gap. We need power and motivation to do God's will. A lot of times, we know what God wants, but we just do not want to do it. We do not feel like doing it, because it takes too much time, money and effort. But, we know that not everyone who says "Lord, Lord" will enter the Kingdom of heaven. How do we move from knowing God's will to doing God's will? James says that if we only hear the Word but do not do it, we deceive ourselves (Jas. 1:22). We think that we are Christians, but when we face the Lord, we are going to be surprised. We deceive ourselves, because we hear the Word of God but we do not do it.

Function of grace   What is going to motivate us to do the will of God? There is one beautiful word in the Bible. I love it in all languages, especially in Chinese. It is Ên-tien 恩 典 (grace). To enter God's Kingdom, we need Ên-tien. To be saved, to be born again and to be a Christian—it is all by grace.

To serve the Lord and to live in His power, we need grace. Grace is such a common word we see it everywhere in the Bible. But so many of us do not really know its meaning.

The apostle Paul knew about grace, and he really experienced grace. He was saved by grace. On his way to Damascus to persecute Christians, the risen Lord Jesus met him and saved him. Paul was the one who wrote "For by grace you have been saved" (Eph. 2:8) and "justified. . .by His grace" (Rom. 3:24). He was the one who experienced sufficient grace. If there was anyone who knew and experienced grace, it was the apostle Paul. He also helps us very much to understand grace.

Turn with me to what Paul wrote about grace in 1 Corinthians 15:10:

> But by the grace of God I am what I am, and His grace toward me did not prove vain; but I labored even more than all of them, yet not I, but the grace of God with me.

How many times is grace mentioned in this verse? Three times! This must be a pretty important verse to let us know about grace, since it is mentioned three times. When grace is upon our lives, three things will happen.

a. I know who I am Firstly, "by the grace of God, I am what I am." If the grace of God is with us, we know who we are. In verse nine of this chapter, the apostle said, "I am the least of the apostles." "I am not fit. I am not qualified to be an apostle. I persecuted the Church of God." Paul was there when they stoned Stephen. He persecuted and killed Christians. He was not fit to be an apostle. The Lord knew that. The Lord knows you and me. You do not feel qualified; you do not feel that you are successful; you are a sinner. The Lord knows that. The Lord is never surprised. Do you ever think that the Lord is surprised? He knows everything. You will never catch the Lord say, "Oh, oh. . ." The Lord knows everything, and the Lord knows your background. Grace came upon Paul though he was the least of the apostles. He was not qualified, yet, in verse ten the very first words are "but by the grace of God." When grace is there, you know who you are. No matter who you were in the past, you know who you are now.

Today, so many people do not know who they themselves are. They try to pretend to be whom they are not. There are people who are always proud and boastful of who they are. There are people who try to cut down other people and criticize other people to make themselves feel good. There are people who always tell jokes and make fun, but never truly reveal their true selves. There are people who are busy doing this and doing that in the church to redeem the guilt inside them, for they do not think that there is any good in themselves at all. All these are symptoms of an inferiority complex. But when grace comes, you know who you are. I know that I am a sinner. I know that I have done wrong things. And I know that I am not qualified to be a pastor, but God has called me. God has called you to continue to live for Him, because His grace is upon you and you know who you are.

b. I know what I should do Secondly, "His grace toward me did not prove vain" (v.10). Grace accomplished, in Paul's life, what it was supposed to. Paul's life had meaning, purpose and value. Grace did not prove to be vain—it got Paul on the right direction. Therefore, the second thing about grace is this: When grace is there, you know not only who you are but also what needs to be done. You know where you are going, and you know what you have to do. Grace was there in Paul's life. If grace is in your life, you will have direction and you will know what you ought to do.

c. I know how to do it   Thirdly, Paul said, "I labored even more than all of them, yet not I, but the grace of God with me" (v.10). Because of grace, Paul worked harder than all the apostles. This word "labor" in the original is the real hard toil that sheds sweat, tears and blood. He labored more than any other apostle, because of the grace of God. That is the third thing about grace. When grace is in your life, you know who you are; when grace is in your life, you know what needs to be done; when grace is in your life, you know how to do it. You can work, and work, and work and you will not be tired. You work and work, and you do not complain, because you know it is not you. It is you, but it is not you—it is the grace of God. If you are complaining, or if you feel you just cannot do anymore, you need more grace. So when grace is there, there is no complaint. When grace is there, you work harder than everyone else. When grace is there, you know how to do it. Oh, wonderful grace!

Grace is, if you sum it up into a definition, a power and a desire to do God's will. That is what bridges the gap from knowing God's will to doing God's will. Grace comes in to bridge the gap, then you have the power and the desire to do God's will. If you really love the Lord, you want to serve Him and you have the power to do so. That is God's grace!

Violation of grace   Grace can be violated and grace can be abused.

a. Receiving grace in vain   Turn with me to 2 Corinthians 6:1 and you will see how grace is abused here:

> And working together with Him, we also urge you not to
> receive the grace of God in vain —

It is possible to receive God's grace in vain. The context of this verse is found in 2 Corinthians 5:21, which says that the Lord Jesus died for our sins. He "who knew no sin" became sin on our behalf. This is His love to us. We depend upon what He has done, and this is grace. He did it for us and He bestowed His grace upon us, that we would receive Him. But, it is possible to receive grace in vain.

There is an urgency in this matter because it says in 2 Corinthians 6:1 "we also urge you." Then in verse two, he quoted, from the book of Isaiah written 700 years before Christ, a passage talking about the acceptable time and the day of salvation. Isaiah prophesied of a day to come when there will be salvation for all people, Jews and Gentiles alike. What the apostle was saying here in 2 Corinthians is that, right now, you and I are living in fulfillment of "that day" which Isaiah prophesied long ago. The day is drawing to a close, and there is not much time left. That is why we urge you to receive the grace of God. Grace is available to everybody. Jesus Christ died for our sins and the sins of the world. You have heard of that, your heart is stirred and your emotion is touched. But if you do not act upon it, it is no good. You will still perish with all the unbelievers, because you are still one of them.

But there are some who receive grace in vain. Do not receive the grace in vain! You truly have received grace if your heart has changed. If you are really saved by grace, then there is power and desire within you to do the will of God, to read the Bible, to go to church, to sing hymns, to pray and to witness. If you have not changed or you have no desire and no power to follow God's will, we really doubt your salvation. Maybe you have received grace in vain. You need to repent and receive Jesus Christ as your personal Savior, so that grace will be there to change your life.

b. Nullifying grace Another violation of grace can be found in Galatians 2:21:

> I do not nullify the grace of God; for if righteousness comes through the Law, then Christ died needlessly.

Here is a person who nullifies grace. "Nullify" means to set grace aside, to neglect, to disregard, or to put aside. This is a person who tries to establish his own self-righteousness. He begins in the Spirit, but now he tries to be perfected by the flesh. We need continual grace. Grace is not only at the beginning of our salvation, but grace is also to carry us through our whole life.

There are people who nullify grace, set grace aside, and try to work out what they need to do by themselves. They set up their own rules and regulations, thinking that if they do certain things, those things will make them more spiritual. There are people who will go to the other extreme, thinking that they do not need any rules or regulations. Both of them are nullifying grace. Some feel that they have to attend certain meetings in the church. If they do not do that, they are not spiritual. That is not true. Then, some people say that they do not have to attend any meetings at church, and that they can worship God in the forest. That is not true either. It is one extreme over the other. Both are nullifying grace.

When one nullifies grace, grace becomes ineffective. There is no more joy, no more freedom, and everything is obligation and routine. They have lost grace. Grace is there, but it is ineffective because they set it aside. Have you lost power and desire to do the will of God? You remember you used to have it. If you have nullified grace, then you must get it back.

c. Coming short of grace A very serious violation of grace is found in Hebrews 12:15:

> See to it that no one comes short of the grace of God; that no root of bitterness springing up causes trouble, and by it many be defiled . . . .

That is more serious than the others. A person can not only receive grace in vain, not only nullify grace, but also come short of God's grace. When it happens, there is a root of bitterness and hatred which affects other people. It is a root that digs in deep. This is very serious.

Esau is given as an illustration in verse sixteen. The Bible says that Esau was immoral and godless. Do you remember Esau and Jacob? Esau came back very hungry while Jacob was cooking. Esau said, "Give me some of that food. I am hungry." And Jacob said, "Okay. First, sell me your birthright. Give me the right of the first born. Ah, let me have the inheritance." Esau did not care about the inheritance. He was hungry! He did not care about those things. What good were those things to him now? All he knew was that he was hungry. "Take my birthright. Take my inheritance. I don't care about those things. Just satisfy my stomach now!" So Esau lost his inheritance.

That is what happens when a Christian comes short of the grace of God. He does not care about the inheritance, he does not care about the Kingdom of God, and he does not care about the second coming of Jesus Christ. All he wants to do is to satisfy his desires now, and so he comes short of the grace of God. The Bible says in verse seventeen, that Esau

> was rejected, for he found no place for repentance, though
> he sought for it with tears.

He even cried for it and tried to repent, but it was too late. Let it not be too late for you. Maybe you have come short of the grace of God. You do not care about the Kingdom, you do not care about the crown, and you do not care that the Lord is coming again. All you care about is the "now" or your own drives, lusts and desires. You have no power and no desire to serve God. You come short of the grace of God.

Appropriation of grace   But how do we get grace? You do not want to violate grace, and you want to get back on the right track. How does grace come to us? That is something you and I need to know. Grace is all around; grace is everywhere. This is the age of grace, but grace may still not come to you unless certain conditions are present.

a. For the hurting In 2 Corinthians chapter twelve, we see that the apostle Paul had a thorn in his flesh. This was God's doing, although it says in verse seven that it was a messenger of Satan. The purpose was to keep Paul from exalting himself. That happens in our lives too. There may be thorns in our flesh—things that hurt. They may be from Satan, but God allows them. Just as in Job's life, Satan has to get permission from God before afflicting you and me. God allows thorns to come to keep us humble. You and I need that. Paul prayed three times that his thorn might go away. God said, "Yes, I'll answer your prayers, but not according to your way." That is how God answers our prayers many times. His answers will be beyond our expectations. God says, "My grace is sufficient for you." Grace comes when you are hurting. Some of you are hurting today with different kinds of thorns: maybe sickness, maybe people hurting you, or maybe you have other kinds of thorns. But when you are suffering, grace is there, sufficient and abundant for you.

God is always seeking to stretch us that we may be more trained and more developed. When sufferings come, we will then enter with expectation to overcome, because God is just about ready to bestow His grace upon us. If you give up, grace will not come. If you hang in there, grace will come. You will have power and desire to do God's will. If God's will is for you to suffer, you will be able to do it. God is always trying to stretch us.

Some people say, "I won't go to prayer meeting. I don't have time." "I won't serve the Lord. It's not convenient."

Brothers and sisters, the Lord wants to stretch you. If you do not do God's will until you have time and you do not do God's will until it is convenient for you, then where is God? You do those things in your own power. You do those things because you have time. No one can see the resource of God. Yes, you do not have time, you do not have the effort or the power, and you are very busy. But when God gives you something to do and you do it, it is sacrifice, it is suffering and it hurts. That is when you are going to see God's grace. This is true. When you know that something is God's will for you to do and you do it—even though it may hurt, affliction may come and you may encounter thorns—that wonderful grace will come. I am not saying that it is easy, but you will have power and desire to serve the Lord.

Are you hurting in any way? If you are, then congratulations, because God's sufficient grace is on its way. You feel very weak. Praise the Lord! The power of God can be seen in your weak life. Paul received sufficient grace and he was able to overcome. And now he would rather boast about his weaknesses that the power of God might dwell in him. You have weak areas in your life. Praise the Lord! Go ahead and serve Him. When things happen and when things are accomplished, everyone will know that it is not you because you could not have done it. It is God's grace.

b. *For the humble*   Turn with me to James 4:6:

> But He gives a greater grace. Therefore it says, "GOD IS OPPOSED TO THE PROUD, BUT GIVES GRACE TO THE HUMBLE."

Is it not wonderful that God gives us greater grace? You think that the grace in your life is exhausted. There is no more hope for you. You have no power nor desire whatsoever to serve the Lord, and grace can never come back. But, God gives us greater grace. As it says in the book of John, there is "grace upon grace." Just when you think that grace is gone, grace is there. But it is only for the humble, for God opposes the proud. If you are proud, God opposes you.

Pride is not just boasting about yourself. That is not the only pride. At the beginning of chapter four of James, you see the pride of this church—all kinds of quarrels and conflicts; all kinds of lusts, anger, bitterness, and envy; the lack of prayer and praying with wrong motives; friendship with the world and hostility toward God. This is pride. If you are like that, you are friends of the world. You have bitterness toward people; you have envy inside; and you have fights and conflicts all the time. God will oppose you. If you want to get to know God, He will not let you because you are too proud. He resists you, because He gives grace to the humble.

How do you humble yourself? It says in verse seven, "Submit therefore to God." Submit to the authority of God: God's Word, God's leaders and God's Church. Submit to Him. Wives, you have to submit to your husbands. Children, you have to submit to your parents. Husbands, you have to submit to God directly. Every person needs some authority. That keeps you humble. If you are your own man, you are your own boss; and if you do not have to report to anybody or submit to anyone, you will be proud. God opposes you and you will find no grace, no power and no desire to do God's will. You will not enter the Kingdom of God. "Resist the devil and he will flee from you" (Jas. 4:7). If you do not submit to God, then you are inviting the Devil. It is only when you submit to God, then you are resisting the Devil. Without humility, there is no grace and no desire to do God's will. The one who will be the greatest in the Kingdom is the one who learns to be a servant of all. Humble before God and humble before others.

How do you humble yourself before other people? It is

not by lowering yourself saying, "Oh, no, I'm no good. I can't do anything." You have people all around you and you "lower" yourself. That is not humility; that is false humility. Can you imagine that when a man came to the Lord begging, "Jesus, please come and heal my son. He's sick." Jesus Christ, the most humble of all would say, "Oh, no, no! I can't. I can't do it. I am only the Son of God. I can't do that." That was not how Jesus Christ acted. Jesus knew that He was the Son of God.

Philippians chapter two tells us how to be humble. We look out not only for our own personal interests, but also for the interests of others (Phil. 2:4). We regard others more highly than ourselves. That is true humility. We do not lower ourselves under people around us, otherwise nobody gets lifted up. But by the grace of God, we know who we are, and we are in the business of lifting up everybody above us. We do not lower ourselves under them, but we know exactly who we are. That is how to be humble. If you are not humble, God opposes you. But if you are humble, the grace of God will come and God will give you grace upon grace that you will be able to serve the Lord.

c. For the holy Grace is not only for the ones who are hurting and the ones who are humble but also for the ones who are holy. James 4:8 says:

> Draw near to God and He will draw near to you. Cleanse your hands, you sinners; and purify your hearts, you double-minded.

You must be clean. "Cleanse your hands" means "cleanse your conscience." There should be no guilt in you. If there is guilt residing in your conscience, no grace will come. If you want to keep the guilt in you, or if you want to keep the sin in you, God will oppose you and there will be no grace. Cleanse your hands, purify your hearts and be sure of your motives of all your doings. Do you have pure motives in what you are doing? Are you coming to church to worship God, or do you have other motives in mind? When you serve the Lord, do you really want to serve the Lord, or are you just serving your self-interest and showing off to other people?

"Purify your hearts, you double-minded" (v. 8). "Double-minded" means having two souls. You have two intellects, two emotions and two wills. You think one way in the world, but when you come to church, you think in a different way. In the world, you have a lot of pleasures and feelings; when you come to church, you look nice and you have different kinds of emotions. In the world you want to do a lot of things; when you come to church, you know that you should do the things of God. You have two souls! That is what it means by being double-minded. God opposes you, and there is no grace for you. No wonder you have no power and no desire to serve the living God. A Christian must be single-minded: All for Jesus, all for Him and serving Him. Then, God's grace will come.

It is not enough to know God and His will. It is not enough to be tickled by the sermon. A person has to act upon the Word of God. That can only come by grace, for grace gives the power and the desire to do the will of God. Do not violate grace: Do not receive it in vain, do not nullify it, and do not come short of it. If we humble ourselves, then God will not resist us but give us his grace. And when grace comes, we know who we are, we know what needs to be done and we know how to do it.

SPIRITUAL WARFARE

For though we walk in the flesh, we do not war according to the flesh, for the weapons of our warfare are not of the flesh, but divinely powerful for the destruction of fortresses. We are destroying speculations and every lofty thing raised up against the knowledge of God, and we are taking every thought captive to the obedience of Christ, and we are ready to punish all disobedience, whenever your obedience is complete. (2 Cor. 10:3-6)

The Spiritual Warfare

There is a great battle going on: It is a spiritual battle. The apostle tells us that "though we walk in the flesh, we do not war according to the flesh." We are in a spiritual warfare and the weapons are divinely powerful. These weapons can destroy fortresses, speculations and all kinds of philosophies. They can take into captivity every thought to the obedience of Christ.

Not physical battles Battles have been fought all over the world and throughout the ages. Here in the twentieth century, we have had the most wars in human history. We see these wars not just as physical wars, but as wars spurred on by political ideologies like Communism, Fascism and Nazism. Battles are going on in different homes and in different families. People isolate themselves from society. There is a battle going on in the morals of Man. People do not know what is right and what is wrong anymore. What used to be wrong yesterday is fine today. There are also battles going on in religion, in education and in all kinds of things. These battles are only a manifestation of a deeper root problem—the spiritual battle. That is why we Christians fail so much, because we are trying to fight them on a carnal, fleshly level.

Not carnal weapons We need to know what the enemy is throwing at us before we know how to counterattack. If the enemy is coming at us with tanks, what do we use to fight back? Do we take out a knife and try to attack the tank? We do not do that. If the enemy is coming at us with jet planes and fighting us from the air, we cannot fight him with kung-fu 功夫 (marshal art). That is the wrong counterattack. We Christians have become so ignorant of what the enemy is throwing at us. We do not even realize that it is a spiritual battle. We think that the battle is the fight we had with our friends or the fight we had with our wives. We think that the battle is the problem we had with our jobs or our children. We do not realize that there is a deeper root problem, because we are fighting with the weapons of the flesh.

Not against blood and flesh In Ephesians chapter six, God tells us where we can get divinely powerful weapons. The apostle Paul writes about the riches we have in Jesus Christ and the great salvation through faith by the grace of God. Then he writes about the Church. Oh, the beautiful

Church of God! After that he speaks about the relationship between husband and wife, and parents and children. When he comes to Ephesians 6:10, he says, "Finally," because he knows that after all has been said, these beautiful things can come to ruination if the spiritual battle is lost.

Paul says in verse twelve that our struggle is not against flesh and blood. In the original language, it is "our struggle is not against blood and flesh." Of course, we do have the flesh, our old nature, and we do have to struggle with our flesh, yet the Bible is not talking about that here in this passage. This verse is telling us that our struggle is not with blood and flesh. In other words, our struggle is not a physical thing, but a much deeper one, a spiritual struggle. The word "struggle" is like a wrestling match which is one on one. Two people are wrestling in close contact. What is the close conflict you are having personally? You need to understand that it is not just with your blood and flesh, and it is not what you see with your eyes. It is a deeply rooted invisible warfare.

The Satanic Kingdom

> For our struggle is not against flesh and blood, but against the rulers, against the powers, against the world forces of this darkness, against the spiritual forces of wickedness in the heavenly places. (Eph. 6:12)

"Against" is mentioned five times here. This shows us the intensity of the conflict. There is something deeply rooted in the spiritual warfare which you and I as Christians better be aware of. This battle is not against some abstract evil in the world. Here, the Bible talks about "rulers," "powers," "world forces of this darkness" and "spiritual forces of wickedness in the heavenly places." This is the kingdom of Satan. Satan's kingdom is highly sophisticated and well organized. Do not think of Satan as a Devil in a red suit with horns and a pitchfork. He has all kinds of demonic forces which are highly sophisticated and organized.

Rulers "Rulers" are demons who have different domains. They are in control of different places. There is a demon in control of the United States, and another in control of the Soviet Union. We know that from the book of Daniel. There were demons in charge of the kingdom of Persia and there was a greater demon behind the king of Babylon. Some demons are in charge of families and some are in charge of individual persons. Each of these demons has been assigned to a domain. They are "rulers."

Powers There are "powers" for the demons, so they have different kinds of authority. Some demons can make people sick; some can possess people and make them do different things; and some can do all kinds of things.

World forces The "world forces of this darkness" are demons who are here on this earth. It is right where you and I are living now. They have nothing to do with the light but this darkness now.

Spiritual forces "Spiritual forces of wickedness in the heavenly places" are demons who are in the air. They are in the heavenly places; they have conflict with the angels of God. In the book of Daniel, Daniel was praying to God. Much later, then, Gabriel came and he told Daniel:

> your words were heard, and I have come in response to your words. But the prince of the kingdom of Persia was withstanding me . . . . (Dn. 10:12-13)

Even the archangel Michael had a contest with Satan over the body of Moses.

There are demons all around us with all kinds of powers and all kinds of authorities. Satan is not afraid to throw them all at each individual. Satan knows exactly who we are and how we will respond to different situations, for he knows human nature. He cannot read our minds because he is not God, yet he can make a pretty good guess, since he has been around observing human nature for a long time. He knows our weakness. He knows how to attack us, how to discourage us and how to get us down spiritually. He will use physical things. We should not be ignorant of his devices, because we have the Bible and the Bible tells us that our struggle is not with blood and flesh, but with all the forces of Satan.

The Evil Day

There are many of you who are having big conflicts now. I know some of our young people whose parents are on the brink of divorce. Some of you are having struggles in your jobs. There are personality struggles, relationship problems, anger, bitterness, jealousies, and critical spirits. We need to realize that it is not what we see but it is a deeper spiritual struggle. Some of you have no conflict now. Then, this is the time for you to prepare for the conflict, because I guarantee you that that day will come.

Satan will attack you   It says in Ephesians 6:13:

> take up the full armor of God, that you may be able to resist in the evil day . . . .

This is a specific day of evil, when all the forces of Satan are going to come upon you. This is not the day of Armageddon, or the day of your death, or the day of tribulation, but this is a specific evil day every single Christian will have to face. If you are not facing anything now, this is the time God has granted you to prepare for that evil day. Some of us may have, perhaps, several evil days. This is the time to prepare and put on the full armor of God. This armor of God is our spiritual weapon.

Put on God's armor People are putting on different kinds of armors and different kinds of protective devices, but not the armor of God. They will be like straw in the face of the enemy. When there is conflict, some put on the armor of withdrawal. They do not want to do anything with it. Some put on the armor of a mask, hypocrisy. Some put on the armor of self-determination, "I'll fight it myself." These are armors of the flesh and they will for sure fail. Some put on the armor of education, "I'll be highly educated, then I can fight any battle in this world." Some of you students do not realize that you are being brainwashed in your secular education. Satan is behind education. That is what we call "secular humanism," which means—"with what I learn from education, I can solve all the problems in the world, because Man can do it. I do not need God." Satan is behind our educational systems. Man cannot solve the problems and that is what happens with education. This is the wrong kind of armor.

The Defensive Weapons

Only spiritual armor can fight the spiritual warfare. There are seven weapons in the armor of God: Truth, righteousness, gospel of peace, faith, salvation, Word of God and prayer (Eph. 6:14-18). We see the imagery of a soldier in the armor.

Girdle of truth First of all, in verse fourteen, it talks about how we need to put on the girdle to gird our loins with truth. This is the waist belt that is put on before the armor is put on. This is the belt that holds the scalper and the sword. After the soldier puts on the belt, he hooks on the breastplate that holds up the armor. So this belt is important because it undergirds the whole armor. It is the foundation for the whole armor. We need truth as our undergarment—the girdle every soldier needs. Do you believe in the truth of God? Do you believe in God? If you do not believe in God, you have no foundation. You must believe in God. You must believe that our God is all powerful: He is all the truth and He is sovereign. The God we believe in is the same God in the Bible. We need truth, and because of truth our lives become truthful. Do you have sincerity, integrity and honesty? That is truth. That needs to be in the life of a Christian. Without truth as your belt, your whole armor is going to fall apart.

Breastplate of righteousness It is a specific kind of righteousness that can only be found in Jesus Christ through His life and His death. That is the only way we can achieve righteousness. All our hope to get into heaven is on Jesus Christ. Is that true? Without Him, we do not have the breastplate of righteousness. We try to do it by ourselves. We try to do good works to get to heaven. That is self-righteousness and it will never work. Satan will pierce through that so easily. But when our faith and trust is on Jesus Christ and His righteousness, there is no piercing of the armor. The breastplate hooks onto the belt and covers all the vital organs, especially the heart. Is your heart covered with the precious blood of the lamb? On what or on whom are you depending on to get to heaven? Put your hope and trust totally upon Jesus Christ.

Shoes of the gospel of peace Then, verse fifteen talks about having shod the feet "with the preparation of the gospel of peace." Our first thought might be that we need to spread the gospel, do evangelism. But this does not fit the context here. Paul is saying how we need to be like a Roman soldier who stands firm on the ground. The kind of sandals the Roman soldiers wore was sturdy with hobnails to ensure a better traction. It is like the athletes today who wear cleats under their shoes, so that they can really have a better grip on the ground. We need to have something that will make our feet sturdy, so that we can stand firm on our ground against the enemy. What that is, is the preparation of the gospel of peace. What gives us courage, motivation and eagerness to stand on our ground? That which prepares our hearts is the gospel of peace. When was the last time you reflected upon the gospel, the good news? There ought to be peace in your heart.

I have no fear what man may do unto me, because whether I live or whether I die I am the Lord's. It does not matter what happens to me. I heard a radio preacher make the following statement, and I agree with him wholeheartedly:

> As long as I am the Lord's and I am on the earth according to God's will as He wants me here, I don't have to fear. I am immortal here on earth until the Lord wants to take me home.

There is great peace. Is that true in your heart? Is it not ironic that before you can wage a great conflict against Satan, you have to have peace in your heart?

Shield of faith And then verse sixteen says, "take up the shield of faith." Oh, how we need that faith. This faith is objective faith, not subjective faith. It is the faith of the Bible. That is what the Bible teaches. It is not what I believe or how I feel about the faith. So again, it is not the shield of my feelings: Sometimes I do not believe; sometimes I do not feel like believing; sometimes I do not feel like a good Christian; sometimes I do not feel like praying; and sometimes I do not feel like reading the Bible. That is not the shield we take. The shield of faith is the faith of the Bible—who Jesus is, who God is and what God says. Do you remember Eve in the garden? She was tempted by the serpent. He attacked her by causing doubts to come into her mind. She tried to answer back with her own thinking, so she failed. Then later on Satan tempted Jesus Christ. How did Jesus extinguish Satan's missiles? Jesus said, "It is written!" Jesus had confidence in the Word of

God. Our shield of faith is what the Bible teaches.

Sometimes I do not understand what the Bible says. But it does not make that much difference whether I understand it or not, because it is true anyway. So we are not to rely upon our own feelings, but to take up the shield of faith. That is what is able to extinguish Satan's flaming missiles. "Flaming missiles" connotate things like arrows or darts that can be thrown. Roman soldiers would take an arrow, dip it in some liquid, set the tip of the arrow on fire, and then shoot the arrow at the enemy. Although that flaming arrow is only a small fire, it will set everything ablaze if it hits its target. Some of us have been hit with those flaming missiles. A little anger can set afire a great bitterness toward people. A little flaming arrow of lust can explode the fiery passion of a man. Flaming missiles have hit each one of us. If we put our faith in the Faith that extinguishes those little arrows, then they will never catch fire in our hearts. We need the shield of faith.

Helmet of salvation Then it talks about the helmet of salvation in verse sixteen. This helmet is the salvation which protects the head. The shield protects the whole body, but a person still has to look over the shield to see what is going on. Do you have the hope of salvation? Are you assured of eternal life? If you are, then you can be a soldier of Christ. You can lift your head with confidence and joy, and nothing can take you away from standing your ground before the Lord. We need the helmet of salvation. It is the emblem that we belong to the Lord.

The Offensive Weapons

Sword of the Spirit Verse seventeen talks about the sword of the Spirit, which is the Word of God. The sword comes from the Spirit of God. It is the spiritual word and it is the Word of God. This word is <u>rhēma</u>. One time, Dr. Lin preached on <u>rhēma</u> ῥῆμα (the spoken Word of God) versus <u>logos</u> λόγος (the written Word of God). It is not merely the cold written facts of the words, but the spoken Word, the words that have life and have meaning. The sword of the Spirit is the utterances of God. When we share the Word of God, it has to have life and it has to have meaning in what we do. When we share with people, we do not just share cold facts "that is what the Bible says." We need to put meaning and life to the very Word, the utterances of God. This is a very powerful weapon which can be used as defense as well as offense. Like any dangerous weapon, you have to practice using it. The Word of God is sharper than any two-edged sword. If you do not practice, you may cut yourself. Become skillful with the Word of God so that when that evil day comes upon you, you will know how to use it.

Prayer and petition Then finally, there is the offensive weapon of prayer. Ephesians 6:18 says:

> With all prayer and petition pray at all times in the Spirit,
> and with this in view, be on the alert with all perseverance
> and petition for all the saints . . . .

The word "all" is mentioned four times. It shows you the significance of prayer. Here it says "prayer" and "petition." The word "prayer" is a general word for the prayer we pray to God. But the word "petition" includes supplication and intercession. It is a special prayer, an intense prayer. We need to be on the alert with all perseverance and petition for all the saints. You see, brothers and sisters, we are in this warfare together. But you and I have to fight our own warfare single-handedly. Nobody can fight the battle for you or for me. But what we can do and what we ought to do is to be on the alert for our brothers and sisters, who are fighting on different lines and on different fronts of the battle. I cannot fight his battle because I am fighting my battle. But even as I am fighting my own battle, I need to be on the alert and see if my brother is in trouble. I need to help him and I need to pray for him. This is an offensive weapon which we can do things with.

But, like the sword of the Spirit, we need to practice using it. We have to become skillful with this offensive weapon of prayer, and to learn how to supplicate, how to petition, and how to intercede for others. How are you going to practice this? This is what our prayer meeting is for. You ought to be there to learn how to pray like that. We can be a church that is on the watch, on the alert for one another in prayer. Let us not only be concerned with our own spiritual battle but also be on the alert for others.

The Triumphant Strategy

Be strong in the Lord The Lord has given us not only the weapons and the armor but also the strategy for victory. Let us go back to Ephesians 6:10. It says, "Be strong in the Lord." This verb is in the passive voice, so it means "let the Lord make you strong." You cannot make yourself strong. Maybe you feel weak today, and you feel discouraged. Then, praise the Lord, because the apostle Paul says, "When I am weak, then I am strong" (2 Cor. 12:10). Be strong in the Lord. Our responsibility is to stay and remain in the Lord, to be close to Him, to be quiet and to listen to Him. The Bible says, "In quietness and trust is your strength" (Is. 30:15). It is God's responsibility to make us strong. God knows how to do it. The Bible says that He has strength, He has might and He has all kinds of resources to give us the power we need. When we are in the Lord, the Lord will make us strong.

Put on the full armor Verse eleven says, "Put on the

full armor of God," and verse thirteen says, "take up the full armor of God." Putting on the armor of God is our preparation; taking up the full armor of God means we are ready to fight. It is time for many of us to put it on. We are ready to practice and ready to fight. The Bible asks us to put on the full armor of God. Many Christians have only put on partial armor. They have all the defensive mechanisms but not the offensive weapons. That is no good. You need both. When you play a sport, you have to play defense and offense; otherwise, you will lose the game.

We need the full armor of God. Maybe you have truth and you have the shield of faith, but you are not sure if you are going to heaven, because you have no helmet of salvation. Satan will strike a blow to your head. Or maybe, you have the belt of truth and the breastplate, but you do not have the shield of faith. Those flaming missiles will pierce your armor. You have no way to extinguish those flames. Put on the "full armor of God." If you are vulnerable somewhere, you are vulnerable enough to be crippled. Satan knows where to pierce. Is there any vulnerable spot in you? Do you have doubts about God's Word? Is there a lack of truth in your belt? Do you really trust in God's Word? Do you have peace in your heart? How can you fight the battle? Put on the full armor of God.

Stand firm continuously And finally, the last strategy is the phrase "stand firm." Ephesians chapter one tells us how we are sitting with Christ in the heavenly places. That is our position in the Lord. In chapter four, it tells us how we need to walk worthy of our calling. This is our conduct and our behavior. And then we come to Ephesians chapter six, which tells us to "stand firm." Yes, we have a position and we have good conduct, but we must also stand firm. Verse eleven says:

Put on the full armor of God, that you may be able to stand
firm against the schemes of the devil.

The word "schemes" means "methods," the craftiness of
Satan. He has all kinds of strategies; the Devil does. He does
not attack just in one way. He has all kinds of angles to get at
you. We need to be on the alert, put on the full armor of God
and stand firm. Satan may be attacking this way, so I will
stand here right against him. His method or his scheme may be
this way, so I will turn and I will stand there against him this
way. We need to learn how to stand firm. That is the way the
Roman army fought. All ranks of soldiers must stand in one
line and stand firm with their swords, spears and shields.
Never compromise your faith or your morals. Match your faith
with the faith of the Bible.

Verse thirteen says, "that you may be able to resist . . . ."
Look at the word "resist." That means "to stand against." It is
the intense form of the word "to stand." A little more activity
here. Then it continues in verse thirteen, "having done
everything, to stand firm." You put your armor on, you fight
the battle, and you have some victory. Do not let up! Stand
firm! In verse fourteen it says, "Stand firm therefore." This
"stand" is in a different tense, the present tense. It means to
stand firm continuously. Too many Christians have given up!
When they had a sweet smell of victory, just one little victory,
they let down their guard and Satan attacked again. Satan will
initiate wave upon wave of attack. Do not boast the pride of
victory, because the battle is not won until Jesus comes again!
Keep standing firm in the Lord. When you resist the Devil, he
will flee from you.

Do not rely upon your feelings but take up the shield of
faith. Because God has said so, so I believe. My hope is
resting upon God's Word, not upon my feelings. We are

engaged in a tremendous conflict with Satan this day. If Satan has not done so yet, there will come a day in every Christian's life when Satan pours out all his forces upon him. This is an invisible warfare, yet its manifestations are felt in the deepest core of our hearts. God has given us a way to fight, not with the weapons of the flesh, but with the weapons that are spiritual and divinely powerful. You must "be strong in the Lord," you must "put on the full armor of God," and then you must "stand firm." May God help us. Let us remember one another in prayer, for we are all fighting the battle individually, yet together.

WHAT HAPPENS WHEN I SIN?

The anthem sung by our choir today, "There Is a Song in My Heart," is about having a new joy. How every Christian ought to have joy in his heart! But when we really look at ourselves, we wonder, "Where is the joy?" We know that our God wants to give us joy and He desires to bestow blessings upon us, but we need to be willing to receive them. Why do we lack joy? It is not God's fault, for God always wants to give us joy. The problem lies with us.

Christians Can Sin

It is very clear that a Christian can sin. He can sin just as much as an unbeliever. But a Christian ought to know better and have more power to overcome sin, because he knows the way to forgiveness and cleansing. That is the only difference between an unbeliever and a believer. Otherwise, they both are the same. We know what happens to an unbeliever when he sins, but sometimes, we do not understand what it means when a Christian sins. What I want to share today, is a very serious matter.

First, let us remove from our minds a false teaching that says, "a Christian does not sin." The Bible tells us that if we confess our sins, God will forgive us. That word "confess" is in the present tense, which means continual confession and confessing every day. Even the great apostle John included himself when he said, "If we confess our sins . . ." (1 Jn. 1:9). The Lord Jesus told us that we need to ask for forgiveness daily. When He taught us to pray, He said, "forgive us our sins" (Lk. 11:4).

What Is Sin?

The definition of sin Now, what is sin? Romans 3:23 tells us:

> for all have sinned and fall short of the glory of God . . . .

That which does not glorify God is sin. That which falls short of God's standards is sin. If what we are doing in our lives does not glorify God or falls short of His glory, that is sin. So it does not necessarily mean that we have done something morally wrong or bad. If we just sit there and do nothing, that can be sin. For example, the Bible says that we are to make disciples and preach the Word to all nations. If we are not doing that, we sin. God tells us to pray without ceasing. If we do not pray, we sin. The Bible tells us to love God with all our heart, with all our soul, with all our mind and with all our strength. Do you love God like that? If not, that is sin!

You may say, "Well, I don't do anything bad! I just sit at home, drink milk and watch television. I don't hurt anybody." But, in God's eyes, it is sin if we have fallen short of the glory of God. It does not necessarily mean that we have done something "bad"! Even if we are indifferent or if we have unbelief, that can be sin. So, let us clarify it now—sin is not just doing something bad; it can just mean that we sit around too much or we are not serving the Lord. We may not have hurt anybody, but we still hurt God.

The seriousness of sin Sin is a serious matter: it leads to death, it leads to punishment and it leads to hell. Sin is to be hated, because it never helps anybody, never loves anybody and never rewards anybody. We should detest sin and try to avoid sin as much as possible. We must hate sin.

But some people do not care. "It doesn't matter. If I sin, God will forgive me anyway." Brothers and sisters, let us be mature and be adult about it. One day, we shall face the Lord in judgment. If we continue in our sin, let us not make excuses on that day, nor try to justify ourselves, because we know that we have contributed to sin today.

The progression of sin The men of God in the Bible sinned. Moses sinned; Peter sinned; David sinned. I would like us to look at David. He will be our illustration of a godly man who sinned. David was God's chosen one. He was a shepherd boy, who killed the great giant Goliath and later became the king of Israel. Turn to 2 Samuel 11:1-3, where we read of David's sin:

> Then it happened in the spring, at the time when kings go out to battle, that David sent Joab and his servants with him and all Israel, and they destroyed the sons of Ammon and besieged Rabbah. But David stayed at Jerusalem. Now when evening came David arose from his bed and walked around on the roof of the king's house, and from the roof he saw a woman bathing; and the woman was very beautiful in appearance. So David sent and inquired about the woman. And one said, "Is this not Bathsheba, the daughter of Eliam, the wife of Uriah the Hittite?"

a. The steps to initial sin We see here the progression that led him to sin. First of all, he was idle. He stayed in Jerusalem while everybody was out there fighting the battle. He sent everybody else out, but he himself decided to stay. After all, it was springtime, a time to play and a time to have fun. David decided to have some fun. Let us be careful when we decide to have fun. In verse two, we see that he saw a woman bathing. That was the second step that led him to sin. He saw the temptation; he saw something he would like to have. Then it says in verse three that he inquired about the woman. He wanted more information because he started indulging more and more into this sin. So, David fell into sin gradually:

1. He was idle,
2. He saw,
3. He inquired, and
4. He took.

He took her and committed adultery. Bathsheba became pregnant.

b. The steps to subsequent greater sins Now David began to plot. He called Bathsheba's husband, Uriah the Hittite, back from battle. When he returned, David told him, "Go down to your house," for David did not want anyone to know that he was the father of Bathsheba's baby. But Uriah was a loyal soldier to David. He said, "How can I go home to my wife when all my fellow soldiers are fighting the battle?" Uriah would not go. Then David plotted to make Uriah drunk and get him home. But Uriah, even in his drunken stupor, was still loyal to David; he would not go to his wife.

David was getting deeper and deeper and deeper into sin. Finally, he planned to have Uriah killed. He sent a note to the general on the battlefield. The note read: "I want you to have Uriah stand at the front line, have all the other soldiers back away and let him get killed." And who carried this message to the general? It was Uriah himself. Oh, the wickedness of David!

When someone gets into sin, it gets worse and worse and worse. We must stop the sin right at the beginning. As soon as we see it, we have to stop it right there. Sometimes our eyes wander around. We see something we would like to have, and we see something we would like to do. Immediately, we need to stop it right there. But David began to inquire, he wanted more information and he wanted to look some more. If you and I start doing that, we will fall into sin. Once we fall into sin, we will try to cover it up with all kinds of wickedness. David's cover-up ended in the death of Uriah.

The Effects of Sin

On our relationship with God

a. God knows Then God sent His prophet Nathan to David. Nathan told David this story. "There were two men, a rich man and a poor man. The rich man had many sheep, and the poor man had only one little lamb. One day, the rich man had a guest that came to his house. The rich man would not kill one of his own sheep, so he went over and stole the poor man's lamb. He brought the lamb back and killed it for his guest." In 2 Samuel 12:5, it says that after hearing this, David was very angry. He said that the rich man deserved to die. And in verse six he added that the rich man must make restitution for that lamb fourfold. Then looking David right in the eyes, Nathan said, "You are the man!" What a shock it was to David. Somebody knew about his sin! And what a shock you and I will have, when we discover that God knows all our sins. No sin is held secret before God. God actually knows everything.

b. God grieves When we sin, we hurt God. Look at 2 Samuel 12:9:

> Why have you despised the word of the LORD by doing evil in His sight?

When we sin, we despise, we hate and we hurt God. God's honor is hurt, because we have insulted Him, slapped Him in the face and done evil in His sight. As the New Testament puts it, we have grieved the Holy Spirit (Eph. 4:30).

The Bible tells us that if we sin and keep on sinning, God will not hear our prayer. Where is God? God has not moved. God is still everywhere. God is always present. But God cannot answer the prayer of a sinning Christian. If He does, He endorses that sin. So if we remain in sin, our relationship with God will not be good. We will have no joy, and we will not sense the Lord.

c. God judges In 2 Samuel 12:11-14 the Lord's judgment comes upon David:

> Thus says the LORD, "Behold, I will raise up evil against you from your own household; I will even take your wives before your eyes, and give them to your companion, and he shall lie with your wives in broad daylight. Indeed you did it secretly, but I will do this thing before all Israel, and under the sun." Then David said to Nathan, "I have sinned against the LORD." And Nathan said to David, "The LORD also has taken away your sin; you shall not die. However, because by this deed you have given occasion to the enemies of the LORD to blaspheme, the child also that is born to you shall surely die."

We see here that sin is a very serious matter. This sin affected David's household, his wives and his son. His sin was done in secret but his judgment was on public display. Furthermore, verse fourteen says that his sin has given occasion to the enemies of the Lord to blaspheme the name of God.

Please note that in verse thirteen, David confessed his sin

and he was forgiven. Praise the Lord for His grace! When you and I confess our sins, we are forgiven. We really have to praise the Lord that we are forgiven, because we do not deserve it but we are forgiven.

I once read about a drunk named Old Bill. He went into bars, got drunk and picked fights with everybody. One day, Old Bill went to pick a fight, and in that fight he lost one eye. Later on, Old Bill was converted; he received Christ as his Savior. Old Bill had such a joy in his heart that he changed his name to New Bill. So now, New Bill was walking with the Lord. His sins were forgiven. But how many eyes do you suppose New Bill had? He still had one eye. Even though we have been forgiven of our sin, we still must suffer the consequences of that sin.

Two young people get involved in a sexual encounter and the Christian girl becomes pregnant. The boy and the girl feel guilty; they confess their sins before God. God will forgive their sins. Praise the Lord! He forgives sins. But do you suppose that the baby will disappear? There are grave consequences from our sins!

In David's case, he had to pay for his sin. Although he was forgiven, he had to make restitution fourfold. He committed adultery with Bathsheba and killed her husband, Uriah the Hittite. He had to pay fourfold:

1. His baby by Bathsheba died (2 Sam. 12:18).
2. His daughter Tamar was raped by her half-brother Amnon (2 Sam. 13:14).
3. Absalom revolted against David and laid with David's wives (2 Sam. 16:22).
4. Absalom was caught in an oak tree and was killed with three spears in his heart (2 Sam. 18:14).

When you and I sin, we have to confess and we have to make restitution as well. If we truly confess our sin, we also have to pay back. That shows that we have true repentance. But, it is too high a price to pay for sin, so we must hate sin.

On our relationship with others Sin does not necessarily mean that we have done something bad. It can just mean neglecting to do something that we ought to have done. That is falling short of the glory of God. In 1963, there was a letter to the editor of a Dallas newspaper. The letter was written by a Baptist Sunday School teacher. In this letter, the teacher was very sad, because there was a student in his class whom he never reached out for Christ. The student came once in a while, but the teacher just neglected him and did not care much about him. The name of the student was Lee Harvey Oswald, who later assassinated President John F. Kennedy. Five years later, there was another testimony by a teacher in Pasadena, California. There was a dark-skinned boy who attended his Sunday School class. The twelve-year old came a few times and then dropped out. The Sunday School teacher never called him and never visited him. The name of this boy was Sirhan Sirhan, who later killed Robert F. Kennedy.

We who are pastors, deacons, teachers, counselors, mothers and fathers, have tremendous influence upon other people. Our neglect can prove to be a curse to other people. Our sin, falling short of the glory of God, can affect other people. Because of sin, we do not witness. Because of sin, we bear a bad testimony. It causes the enemy to bear reproach upon Christ and blaspheme the name of God. It is our sin, as well as their sin, that leads them to hell. Oh, let us hate sin. Let us fear its grip upon our lives!

On our joy of salvation We see that God struck David's baby. David began to pray and fast. He wept, he lay on the ground and he could not eat. When we sin, we too shall lose the joy of salvation. David wrote:

> Restore to me the joy of Thy salvation, (Ps. 51:12)

He knew that he had salvation. You and I have salvation if we truly believe in Jesus Christ. But the joy is gone because of sin. No wonder Peter wept bitterly after he denied Christ three times. When we sin, God will discipline us. He took away David's baby. How terrible it would be if one of our loved ones is taken away for our discipline. Hebrews chapter twelve tells us why God disciplines us. It is because He loves us— He is a father to us and we are His sons. That is the motivation behind discipline.

Sometimes, my children are bad and I have to punish them. It might mean spanking; it might mean scolding. Afterwards my sons would cry. I would tell them, "I want you to go into your room to cry. I don't want you to cry in front of me." They would cry and sob in their room. When they have calmed down, I would open the door and say, "Have you finished?" "Yes, Daddy." And then I would put my arms around them and sit down. "Do you know what you did?" "Yes, Daddy." We would talk about it, and pray about it. And they would feel the love. Sometimes God has to discipline us to get us out of that sin, but He does it with His arms around us. It is based upon His love. David learned his lesson. He had to pay so much for his sin.

Sometimes God will inflict sickness upon those who sin. It tells us in 1 Corinthians 11:30, how some people took the Lord's supper in the wrong way, that they became weak and sick and some died. Some people died prematurely because of discipline, like Ananias and Sapphira (Acts, chapter five). God will take away some Christians, because they sinned too much. God would rather let them die to stop them from sinning than let them live to continue in sin.

The Conquest over Sin

Confess the sin immediately God's discipline is serious. We must learn the lesson quickly and get out of the sin. David learned well. Look at 1 Kings 15:5:

> because David did what was right in the sight of the LORD, and had not turned aside from anything that He commanded him all the days of his life, except in the case of Uriah the Hittite.

Praise the Lord that David learned well. This verse tells us that David always did right. And the only exception mentioned here is that with Uriah the Hittite. That is why David was a man after God's heart. Even though he had sinned, after this lesson, he learned how to confess his sin and be cleansed right away.

Oh, may we learn our lesson and learn how to really confess our sins. The first thing we should do is to confess our sin immediately. As soon as we recognize that it is sin, we need to confess it immediately. David gave the details of his confession in Psalm fifty-one. Here, David confessed his sin, and we learn something from his confession: We need to confess our sin immediately. What we mean by that is we need to keep a short account with God. Some of us have credit cards, and we get bills. When the bill comes for a credit card purchase, we have a choice to make. Either we pay the whole amount off or we pay a little bit every month. How good it is to pay off the whole amount. When we do not use the credit card, we owe nothing on the bill next month.

Some of you wash dishes; I hope you all wash dishes. How good it is to finish washing all the dishes each night. When you wake up in the morning, the dishes are all clean and the kitchen is clean. But, some people wait. One day goes by, then the next and the next. They never wash the dishes. Then they try to eat something. When they open the cupboard, there are no more dishes for they are piled in the sink. Keep washing consistently. Keep a short account with God. In Psalm 51:1-2, it says:

> Be gracious to me, O God, according to Thy lovingkindness;
> According to the greatness of Thy compassion . . .

We have to know the basis for forgiveness and confession. The Bible mentions three things here. First of all, it is God's grace; secondly, it is God's lovingkindness; and thirdly, it is according to God's compassion. Oh, God's grace is wonderful! Who are you and I that God is so gracious to us? We have hurt His name so many times. We have disappointed Him and we are always falling short of His glory. But God loves us. God is gracious to us. Therefore, we can come to Him freely. Jesus died on the cross! He did not have to die but he wanted to, because He loves you and me. He was willing to die for our sins. Among all the people you know, who will die for you? Whom do you know is willing to be nailed on the cross, so that you and I can have life? Oh, God loves us so much! He calls us to confess our sin and receive forgiveness. So praise the Lord for His grace!

Identify the sin concisely Then we have to identify a sin as a sin. Notice how David confessed his sin in so much detail. He called it an iniquity, a sin and a transgression. In verse four, he writes:

> Against Thee, Thee only, I have sinned,
> And done what is evil in Thy sight,

There was a lady who came up to the great evangelist D. L. Moody years ago. She said, "Mr. Moody, will you please help me? I have a bad habit of exaggerating a lot when I speak to people. I know that I was telling stories, for I put in things that were not really true." D. L. Moody said, "Let me tell you. Next time you do that, you go to that person and confess to him, 'I'm sorry. I told a lie.'" Then she said, "Aw, I wouldn't call it a lie! I just exaggerate." D. L. Moody replied, "If you don't call it a lie, you will never stop."

Let us not trifle with sin. Let us not play games with sin. Call a sin a sin. You have a "bad habit." You will never stop your "bad habit," until you call it a sin. You have to say, "For me, smoking is a sin." "For me, dancing is a sin." "For me, drinking is a sin." You have to call it a sin or you will never stop. Let us not give it a nice name. Let us not make anymore allowances. It says in verse three:

> For I know my transgressions,
> And my sin is ever before me.

David is saying, "I am always reminded of that sin. I'm sick of it and I dislike it. Please get rid of it."

Take the consequences bravely Are you sick of your sins? Are you sick of your so-called bad habits? Oh, maybe you have not hurt anybody, but you have fallen short of God's glory. You have to hate sin, detest sin and get rid of sin! You need God's help. Confess it to God and you will be forgiven. The true confession always means restitution also. If you have cheated someone, you need to confess your sin. Yes, you have to pay back as well. Have you cheated on an examination? Yes, you need to confess it.

A young man confessed to me when I was in Seattle. He felt very bad, because he knew that he had cheated on an examination. I said, "Well it's good you have confessed it. God will forgive you. But you may need to make restitution. You must go back and call your professor, and tell him that you have cheated." "I can't do that!" I said, "Why not? Are you willing to take the consequences? It may mean that you have to take a lower grade." "Well, it's hard for me to do that." "I know it's hard. But that's the consequence you have to pay. Or else, you'll never have peace, and you'll never have joy." The young man did it. He called his professor. "Professor, I cheated on the exam. I'm willing to take a lower grade." But the professor said, "Young man, I want to see you." So he set up an appointment, and they got together. The professor said, "I've been teaching for fifteen years, and no one has ever confessed that he has cheated on my examination. I know that some did." That young man had a testimony for Jesus Christ before the professor.

When we sin, there are consequences. Are you willing to take the consequences? If you have cheated on your taxes, confess and pay back the government, and be willing even to go to jail if necessary. Otherwise, you do not have true confession, you do not have true repentance, and you will never have peace.

Center on God's presence consistently Turn now to Psalm 51:10-12:

> Create in me a clean heart, O God,
> And renew a steadfast spirit within me.
> Do not cast me away from Thy presence,
> And do not take Thy Holy Spirit from me.
> Restore to me the joy of Thy salvation,
> And sustain me with a willing spirit.

There are three things David asked of the Lord: to create a clean heart, to renew a steadfast spirit, and to sustain a willing spirit. David desired to have close communion with God. That is what you and I need. We need time with God. The Bible asks:

> How can a young man keep his way pure?
> By keeping it according to Thy Word. (Ps. 119:9)
> Thy word I have treasured in my heart,
> That I may not sin against Thee. (Ps. 119:11)

The New American Standard Bible says, "Thy word I have treasured in my heart." You and I need a treasury of God's things. It is like a reservoir filled with water, living water. When things become dry, the Holy Spirit will take from the reservoir and quench our thirst. Our reservoir is built up through time with God and memorizing God's Word. As we memorize God's Word, the reservoir is built up. Whenever we have need, the Holy Spirit will apply it and bring that verse or passage up from a study, a sermon or a Sunday School lesson. We will have power to overcome sin.

Are we spending time with God? Without that, we have no reservoir and we have no power. We need to center on God's presence. Then, God will give us victory. It is a day by day activity. If we do that, Psalm 51:13-14 tell us:

> Then I will teach transgressors Thy ways,
> And sinners will be converted to Thee.
> Deliver me from bloodguiltiness, O God, Thou God of my
>   salvation;
> Then my tongue will joyfully sing of Thy righteousness.

Then we will have a testimony and we can lead people to Christ. Because our sins are gone, revival will come and we will have power to tell people about Christ. It is not because we have eloquent words, but because we are clean and the Holy Spirit can work through us to reach other people.

Come to God humbly How can we come to Him? Psalm 51:17 explains:

> The sacrifices of God are a broken spirit;
> A broken and a contrite heart, O God, Thou wilt not despise.

God despises sin and God hates sin, but God never despises our broken heart. He loves to have us come to Him humbly. Christians can sin; and if we remain in sin, there are great consequences. Maybe we are facing some sin right now. We need to confess it immediately. We need to come to God humbly.

> O, for the wonderful love He has promised,
> Promised for you and for me!
> Though we have sinned, He has mercy and pardon,
> Pardon for you and for me.
> Come home, come home,
> Ye who are weary, come home;
> Earnestly, tenderly, Jesus is calling,
> Calling, O sinner, come home!
>
> —Will L. Thompson, "Softly and Tenderly Jesus Is Calling"

THE BATTLE WITHIN

This topic is so applicable to every Christian. If you are not a Christian, you are going to see why you ought to be one. Let me share with you some instances that you can readily identify with. There was a man on vacation, driving about 600 miles. The children in the back were getting very restless because of the long drive. He hit a detour, so it took some time; he had a flat tire, which took more time. Finally, they got to the motel. But they got there too late and the motel gave his reservation to another family. The wife began to yell at him, "Why didn't you call ahead of time?" She yelled other things at him also. What happened to the man? His temper began to explode. He began to yell back at her, at the children and at everybody else. He said words he never said before in his life. Two weeks later, things got worse at home. So finally, he went to see a Christian counselor. What he just could not understand was how such foul language could come out of him. He had been a Christian for fifteen years, serving on the church board and serving as a Sunday School teacher. Was he only fooling himself, thinking that he was a Christian? For all these fifteen years, had he only been living a lie?

There was another instance of a pastor who, for many years, preached about God's love and grace. But when he was at home, he yelled at his wife and his children, so things were miserable at home. How could a pastor be like that? How could he live such a life like that?

A man who had been a Sunday School teacher for many years was out at a social, playing volleyball. He began to get angry at his fellow players and displayed very unsportsmanlike conduct. How could a Sunday School teacher behave like that?

I am sure you can think of many other examples in your own personal life. While you ought to be a Christian, you do not seem to be living like one. So are you truly a Christian or are you only pretending to be one? Let me tell you, if you are truly born again and if you have received Jesus Christ in your life, you are regenerated and you are a Christian.

The Opponents

Inside us there is something that can come out even though we are Christians. Sometimes that thing within us is asleep, but it is easily awaken when there is stress, pressure or pride, and Satan is waiting for the ideal moment to bring it out. Basically, this thing is our old nature inherited from Adam. Yes, we have a true spiritual nature which is a new nature, but we also have an old nature. This is a fundamental truth many Christians do not know—every Christian has two natures inside.

Because these two natures oppose each other, there is a battle going on every moment of our lives. All Christians experience this battle. It does not matter how old we are or how young we are, nor does it matter whether we are a Sunday School teacher or a pastor. This battle within is constant and continuous. Decisions have to be made all the time, but the trouble seems to be most Christians are losing the battle. Let us analyze the situation. First of all, we have these two natures which we call the old nature and the new nature.

The Old Nature

a. Definition The old nature has many synonyms in the Bible. Sometimes, it is called "the flesh." We use the term "carnal" Christian, which means a Christian who is always operating according to his flesh. Romans 7:14 says:

> For we know that the Law is spiritual; but I am of flesh....

"Of flesh" is the same word as being carnal or being fleshly. In Galatians 5:17, the Bible says:

> the flesh sets its desire against the Spirit, and the Spirit against the flesh . . . .

We know that the Corinthian Christians were carnal. They were fleshly, so there were strife, divisions, anger and relational problems in the Corinthian church.

If you look back to Romans 6:6, you will find another synonym called "the old self." "The old man" or "the old self" is used as a synonym for the old nature. Romans 7:17 says:

> So now, no longer am I the one doing it, but sin which indwells me.

The old nature is really the flesh of man. It does not just mean the skin on our body but also the evil thoughts, the attitudes and all that we inherited from Adam. It is the "sin nature." It is corrupt, sinful and always wanting to do bad things. The old nature inside us always wants us to do bad things. Galatians chapter five lists the deeds of the flesh, when it talks about immorality, impurity, sensuality, anger and bitterness.

These are deeds of the flesh and they describe what the old nature is.

b. Hostility toward God Romans 8:6 tells you what happens if you continue in the flesh:

> For the mind set on the flesh is death . . . .

If you are always and only in the flesh, there is death. You do not want to have anything to do with God. You do not want to read the Bible; you do not want to pray; you do not want to go to church; and you do not want to listen to those who talk about God. Verse seven says:

> because the mind set on the flesh is hostile toward God....

You are hostile to God because the flesh does not subject itself to the Law of God for it is not able to do so. A person who is in the flesh cannot submit to God's will because the flesh is not able to do that. So if you are in the flesh, you cannot please God. That is what verse eight says:

> those who are in the flesh cannot please God.

If you are in the flesh and continue in the flesh, you displease God. The flesh is corrupt and disobedient; it is proud and against the work of God; it is hostile to God. Even a Christian can be in the flesh, and those who are not in Christ are in the flesh.

The New Nature

a. Definition The new nature comes from God. Jesus says that you must be born again. When you are born again, you receive a new nature. In fact, the Lord Jesus says in John 3:6:

> That which is born of the flesh is flesh, and that which is born of the Spirit is spirit.

126

All of you who are just born of the flesh, regular human beings, are fleshly and will die. But if you are born of the Spirit, you have a spiritual nature, a new nature. What is this new nature? The Bible says in 2 Corinthians 5:17:

> Therefore if any man is in Christ, he is a new creature; the old things passed away; behold, new things have come.

You have a new nature and you have a new outlook towards life. You have new responses, new goals, a new direction and a new perspective, because you have a new nature. That is what a new nature does.

b. *Partaker of divine nature* Do you know what the Bible says about this new nature? 2 Peter 1:4 says that these things have been given to us that we might become "partakers of the divine nature." The new nature is the partaker of the divine nature. The new nature that you and I have is perfect. It cannot sin. You say, "Well, I always sin." Yes, you do, but your new nature does not sin. Your new nature has been created by God, and what God creates is perfect. It has been created in all holiness and in total righteousness. It is a partaker of the divine nature.

Your new nature has the attributes of Jesus Christ. If there could be a full manifestation of the new nature in you, you would be showing forth the fruit of the Spirit. And those are the attributes of Jesus Christ. The Bible says in 1 John 3:9:

> No one who is born of God practices sin . . . .

If you are born of God, you cannot sin. The passage is talking about the new nature in you. If that new nature could be manifested in your life, you would not practice sin. The new nature is good, holy and righteous. Because it is new, you

127

have new interests, new goals and a new direction. The new nature is a citizen of heaven.

The Warfare

The world is hostile to the new nature while the old nature is at home in the world. As we read Romans chapter seven, we see the great warfare.

Competing for control The old and new natures are fighting against each other. They are aggressively competing over who is going to take over your life. It is a constant battle within. Even the great apostle Paul had a struggle. Romans 7:15 says:

> For that which I am doing, I do not understand; for I am not practicing what I would like to do, but I am doing the very thing I hate.

There is something I know I should do, but I am not doing it; and there is something I hate, but I do. Verse nineteen says:

> For the good that I wish, I do not do; but I practice the very evil that I do not wish.

You see, that is the evidence of a battle that is going on in your life.

Bringing forth despair When that battle is going on, it brings confusion, despair and discouragement. There is such despair in verse twenty-four, "Wretched man that I am!" Many of you are going through the struggle right now. You feel like such a hypocrite. You know that there are things you ought to do as a Christian, but you are not doing them, and there are things you know you should not do, but you are doing them. It brings confusion, despair and discouragement into your life, and you feel like a wretched man.

Paul says, "Who will set me free from the body of this death?" (Rom. 7:24) Do you know what this means? It means that you are going to be continually in this body of death as long as you live in this body, and that the old nature is going to be there. The old nature never goes away. It never reforms and never changes for the better. It will always be fleshly, wicked and evil; and it will always seek to control your life. It will aggressively compete against the new nature. If it is manifested in your life, you will be hostile to God.

The Crucifixion

But the victory is in sight. In verse twenty-five of chapter seven, Paul says:

Thanks be to God through Jesus Christ our Lord!

Jesus is the answer. He died on the cross and our flesh is crucified with Him. If you would accept that and if you would believe that Jesus died for you, then your fleshly old nature will be crucified and be dead. This is another fundamental truth many Christians do not know. Romans 6:6 says that "our old self was crucified with Him." That is what the crucifixion of Christ did for us. If you would receive Christ into your heart and be born again, your flesh is crucified and your old nature is dead.

Old nature is dead Now let us get a good understanding of what it means by "the old nature is dead," because we have just said that the old nature will always be there, it will never change and it will never reform. What does it mean now that the old nature is dead and crucified?

"Death" in the Bible means "separation." Your old nature is now separated from God, but it is still alive to the world. It

129

is dead to things of God, because it is not subject to the Law of God and it is not even able to do so. When your flesh—your old nature—is crucified, your new nature then is alive and responsive to God. Though your new nature is responsive to God and your old nature is crucified with Christ, it does not mean that the old nature goes away. Look at Romans 6:6 again. It says that after we have been

> crucified with Him, that our body of sin might be done away with, that we should no longer be slaves to sin.

This is what the crucifixion has done with our flesh—we are no longer slaves to sin.

Christians are emancipated If you are only in the flesh, you have no choice. You cannot help but be slaves of sin, because all you have is the flesh. But now, when you become a born-again Christian and your flesh has been crucified, you are freed from the slavery of sin. So many Christians do not know that they have been emancipated from sin, and that now as a Christian they have a choice. You can be a slave to sin, but now you have a choice: You do not have to be a slave anymore, and you do not have to let sin reign over your mortal body.

When you are only in the flesh, you do not know God. In fact, you are even hostile to God. When God speaks, you do not want to listen, you do not respond and your heart is hardened. But now you have a new nature and that new nature never sins. That new nature is alive with God; it responds to what God speaks. So as a Christian, there is a choice. Romans 8:12 says:

> So then, brethren, we are under obligation, not to the flesh.

It says here that you are no longer under obligation to the flesh. You used to be, but not anymore.

Praise the Lord! Christ has been crucified. If you believe

that, then your old nature is crucified too and you no longer have to live according to the old nature. You have a choice and you have a way of victory. Just let your new nature take over; then you will have victory, and you will be a good Christian.

The Victory

The problem is we do not know how to let the new nature take over. There are so many of us who live in defeat. Although we have the new nature, it is the old nature that is in control. We may know intellectually that Christ has been crucified for our flesh, but we do not sense any victory in our life. May God bring enlightenment.

The understanding You must be aware that you have two natures. If you are a Christian, you must know that your old nature has been crucified. It is dead to the things of God, but is still alive to the things of the world. God has created a new nature in you, and the new nature is alive to God and dead to the world. It is not the new nature that is tempted. The new nature cannot be tempted; the new nature is perfect. It is the old nature that has been tempted, and the old nature that sins. It is not the new nature that brings on a problem with people, but the old nature that clashes with other people. It is the old nature that thinks evil and seeks to gratify our lusts and desires. And it is also the old nature that brings on loneliness and the feeling of being apart from everyone and even from God. So it is the old nature that takes the joy out of living!

So, first of all, you must be aware that there are two natures, and when you sense that the old nature is creeping up to dominate your life, you should know how to get help from God. But many of you do not even know it. You must realize that you have a choice of which nature will take over your life. Let me share with you a little poem:

131

> Two natures beat within my breast.
> One is foul, the other blest.
> The one I love; the one I hate.
> The one I feed will dominate.

This poem speaks so clearly of what we are sharing. You know that there are going to be two natures in you. But you also know that you have a choice of which one will dominate your life.

The nurturing The way you make your choice is by choosing the one you are going to feed. If you are going to be worldly, then you will feed the old nature. The old nature will consume all you give it, because it is alive and responsive to the things of the world. If you continue taking worldly things into your life, the old nature will grow stronger and stronger and eventually it will be able to dominate your life. The new nature is dead to the things of the world. If you never bring in any spiritual things into your life, the new nature will become starved and weak. There is no way the new nature will dominate your life.

a. Starve the old nature Deny the things of the world entrance into your life, so that the old nature will be starved and become smaller and weaker. Bring in the nourishment and food that will enable the new nature to grow, to develop, and to be strong and mature. Then the new nature will dominate your life and will be manifested. Romans 6:11 says:

> Even so consider yourselves to be dead to sin, but alive to God in Christ Jesus.

You must practice this in your life for, as a Christian, you have a new nature. That new nature is dead to sin but alive to God. "Therefore, do not let sin reign in your mortal body." Verse thirteen continues to say:

> do not go on presenting the members of your body to sin as
> instruments of unrighteousness; but present yourselves to
> God as those alive from the dead, and your members as
> instruments of righteousness to God.

Do not feed the old nature. Feed your new nature. You are not under the Law but under grace. Sin shall not be master over you! By His grace, God has given you this new nature. Therefore, sin shall not be master over you. You have a choice now! But too many Christians today are making the wrong choice, and they are feeding and nurturing the old nature. No wonder they are not good Christians. They cannot help themselves because the old nature so dominates their lives that their entire lives are characterized by sin. Oh! What it would be like if a Christian would feed and nurture his new nature. You have a choice; you can do that.

b. Feed the new nature Do not try to get rid of the old nature or be a better Christian by your flesh. You cannot try to be a better Christian on your own, because by your own power you will fail. If you try to be a Christian by your fleshly power, you are feeding your old nature all the more. The only way you can diminish the old nature is by feeding the new nature. When you begin to do the things of God, you are feeding the new nature. It will become stronger and stronger. There will be a fight: the old nature will reject, will regurgitate, and will not accept anything of God in your life.

The battle Many Christians right here in this room today are on the margin. You feel like such a hypocrite and you are about ready to leave the church. There are some of you here who feel so discouraged that you do not read the Bible and you do not pray anymore. That is exactly one hundred and eighty degrees opposite to what God wants you to do. Do you not know that you are starving the new nature?

If you feel discouraged, you must take in more food that will nurture the new nature. You should pick up your Bible and pray more; you should seek for ways to serve the Lord more. Do something for the Lord, because your old nature is dominating your life right now. Your new nature is so weak. As you do a little Bible study, your new nature gets a little stronger; but your old nature is still dominating and there will be a fight. While the old nature is stronger than the new nature, there will be confusion and depression. But do not give up. Continue on feeding the new nature and starving the old nature, then you will find your new nature dominant in your life more and more. When the old nature is starved and weak, you can put it back into the coffin.

Now, the problem is this: on the one hand you say, "Okay, I am going to start feeding my new nature," but on the other hand you still continue feeding your old nature. So although your new nature is growing, your old nature is growing even more, and they begin to stay in the same ratio and grow at the same rate. You must starve the old nature and feed the new nature only. That is the only way you are going to get rid of the old nature. It does not come by trying to be better. Bring in the nourishment that will help the new nature.

The walk Romans 13:14 says: "put on the Lord Jesus Christ. . . ." How are you going to put on the Lord Jesus Christ and make no provisions for the flesh in regard to its lusts? That is exactly what we are saying right now. Do not feed the old nature and make no provisions for the old nature, but make provisions for the new nature. That is how you put on the Lord Jesus Christ. You need to get rid of this fleshly food. The worldly things will only add and feed to your old nature that will eventually dominate your life.

You must watch out for those parties and dances you are going to. You are feeding your old nature. Your new nature has nothing to do with such things. I want to preach out against fraternities and sororities in colleges and school clubs. They have nothing to do with your new nature. You are just adding nutrition to your old nature. You find yourself compromising your faith. Because your old nature dominates your life, you always fail. Watch out what you read and what you see in movies. Will it feed your old nature or will it feed your new nature?

Conclusion

Feed your new nature—read the Bible, pray to God, come to prayer meeting and serve the Lord—this is the only way to win the battle. Do not fall into Satan's trap by thinking that the best thing for me is to quit church and to stop reading the Bible. Brothers and sisters, you can have victory.

• First of all, be aware that there are two natures. They are fighting to dominate your life.

• Secondly, realize that you have a choice. Because Christ has been crucified, your flesh has been crucified also. And now, you have a choice.

If you are not a Christian today, you do not have a choice. You have to serve sin, because you are in the flesh. Ah, but if you are a Christian, you have been emancipated—you are freed from the slavery of sin and the power of death.

• Begin to feed your new nature.

• Make no provision for the lusts of the flesh.

• Get rid of the flesh by walking by the Spirit.

Walking by the Spirit will nurture your new nature. You might fail, for your old nature is looking for any opportunity to manifest itself. If you confess your sins, you nurture your new nature. If you do not confess your sins, you nurture your old nature. Confess your sins, get right with God, and get back to Bible study.

Brothers and sisters, the victory is in sight. Your old nature will always be there. It will never change, not in three months, nor three years, nor three hundred years. But you have a choice in which one you will feed. The one you feed will dominate. The victory is yours. Jesus has already provided for you. Will you come to Him? Will you live for Him? Then, get rid of those worldly things and victory will be yours.

LORD, INCREASE OUR FAITH!

The Importance of Faith

"Faith needs to be increased!" This is the cry of the disciples who asked Jesus to increase their faith. The word "faith" is used over 240 times in the Bible, and the verbal form "to believe," over 230 times. Since this word is used close to five hundred times, it must be extremely important.

In everyday living Faith is not a mysterious thing. You and I exercise faith everyday. When you sit in a car, you believe that the brakes work. When you come into the sanctuary to sit down on a pew and when you see all the people sitting there, you will not think that they are too heavy. You just believe that it is safe enough, and you sit down.

In science Some of you who are involved in science, whether in study or in work, need faith in science as well. Some people believe that man came from monkeys and that there was an evolution of life, because they found these bones and fossils in different levels or layers of dirt. To believe that that bone belonged here and that bone did not come from over there, they have to have faith. They have to believe that gravity always works and the smallest atomic particle is always the same.

In history We have faith in history as well. Today is somebody's birthday. Sometimes we forget because the calendar changes. But today is his birthday. He is George Washington, the first president of the United States. We believe that there was a person named George Washington, but nobody has ever seen him. Instead of having a photograph of him, we only have paintings; but we believe that there was such a man.

The Basis of Faith

In everyday living we have faith, and we exercise faith all the time. How much more in the spiritual realm we need to have faith! We cannot see God, but we need to believe in Him. To do so, we need faith. How do we get faith? How do we come to really believe in something? How does faith work in our lives?

Based upon experience A lot of times our faith is based upon experience. For example, you sit on a chair because you have sat on many chairs, and all those chairs you sat upon held you up. So, it is reasonable when you come to a new chair, or something that looks like a chair, you just sit on it. I have not seen anybody look at the engineering of a chair to see if there is any loose screws or anything wrong before sitting down. They just sit. So, a lot of times our faith is based upon our experience.

But our experience is not always reliable. In my parents' home we have an old chair. We sat on that chair all the time.

A few years ago, my oldest brother had a baby girl. My parents have six boys. This baby girl is the first grandchild and the first girl, so she is precious to all of us. One day, my oldest brother, her Daddy, took her downstairs to the old chair. Holding her in his arms, he sat down. Just at that moment, the chair broke, so he fell down surprised. Of course, he was still holding the baby, but the baby was scared and began to cry. Grandmother ran down the stairs, and all the brothers ran down the stairs. We saw my brother and the baby girl sitting on the floor. My mother grasped the baby and ran upstairs, and all the brothers ran upstairs, leaving my poor <u>koko</u> 哥哥 (older brother) lying there on the floor! Our experience is not always reliable. We think that the chair will hold us up, but it may not.

Based upon knowledge Sometimes our faith is based upon knowledge. We think that we know something, so we put our faith in it. But the problem is that knowledge changes so much today. Just look at the area of computers. The design of a computer becomes smaller yet it holds more information. Computers are the only commodity that is getting cheaper when everything else is getting more expensive. Nowadays, people can buy a computer cheaper than a television set. Knowledge is changing so much. Our experience, our knowledge and our reasoning power are not totally reliable. This affects our faith. We become more suspicious, a little more cautious and sometimes superstitious.

The Definition of Faith

There are many ways to approach the study of faith. Some being philosophical about it say, "you believe and then you will know"; but others say, "you know and then you will believe." Well, we do not want to get philosophical about faith. Let us just see what the Bible says. I am so happy that the Bible is something I can understand, because some of these philosophers I cannot understand.

Its function   Why do we need faith?   The Bible says very clearly that without faith we cannot be saved. If we do not believe in Jesus Christ as our Savior, we are dead in our sins. That is the primary, important area of faith. The Bible also tells us that without faith we cannot live a Christian life. We need faith when the Holy Spirit guides. We need faith in our prayer. If faith is in Jesus, then he who receives Jesus receives faith and has the victory, because Jesus has overcome the world. There is power in faith. If we have faith, we have power to move mountains, to cast out demons and to witness. With faith, nothing is impossible; without faith, we can never understand the Word of God. The Bible says:

> And without faith it is impossible to please Him . . . .
> (Heb. 11:6)

God is looking for those who have faith. So, faith is vitally important.

Its definition   What is faith?   We have a very famous verse in the Bible to describe faith. It is in Hebrews 11:1:

> Now faith is the assurance of things hoped for, the
> conviction of things not seen.

Faith tells us that we have the assurance and the conviction of something we cannot see. Someone has said that faith enables us to see the invisible, to believe the incredible and to receive the impossible. So through faith, we can see the invisible, believe the incredible and receive the impossible. Oh, there is power in faith!

Faith does not make something be there when it is not. Because we believe does not make it true. One can say, "Oh, I wish I had an ice cream right here. Oh, I want an ice cream right here. I believe it will be right here." But it is not here, because believing in something does not make something true. Only that which is true is true. If something is true but we cannot see it, when we exercise faith in that truth we will know that it is true. No man has seen God. He is invisible, but He is there. If we exercise faith, we will know that He is there. God does not appear because we have faith, for our faith does not make Him more true. He is already there and this is true. The problem is we do not know God and we do not understand God. Only when we put our faith in the true and living God, then we will be able to see, and, then we will have the conviction and the assurance that He is really there. Our faith has to be based upon something that is true. We cannot just believe something that is not true. Our faith has to have an objective truth to it. Where is truth but in God's Word?

a. Assurance of God's promise The Lord brought to my mind the father of faith, Abraham. Why do we say that Abraham is the father of faith? Why did he believe so much? When we look at him, we can get an understanding of what faith really is. In Romans 4:16-17, God gave a promise to Abraham that He would make him a father of many nations, and verse eighteen says:

In hope against hope he believed . . . .

In other words, this is impossible!—he contemplated his own body and asked, "How can I be a father of many nations? I don't even have a son, and I am too old to have a son, and especially my wife is too old to have a son. This is impossible! How can I be a father of many nations?" But because God said so, Abraham believed. God promised, and Abraham believed the promise of God.

We notice here that Abraham did not understand it. He could not fully comprehend, "How can I be a father of many

141

nations? But God said so, so I will believe." This is the truth which is given to us in God's Word. We do not fully understand it; we do not like it; we do not think that it is going to work; and we do not feel like doing it. But God said so, so I will believe. It is impossible, it is incredible and it is unbelievable; but I believe because God said so. You and I need to have the assurance of God's promise. Then, in verse twenty, the Bible says:

> yet, with respect to the promise of God, he did not waver in unbelief . . . .

In spite of circumstances, Abraham believed in God.

b. Assurance of God's power—He can You and I sometimes say, "Well, that's Abraham. I'm me. It works for him and it works for others, but it doesn't work for me." We have heard what God has said and we know that we should act upon it; but when facing a decision, we evaluate our situation, look at our environment and our own abilities—what we can do and what we cannot do—and then, we say, "It is impossible." God says, "Pray, and I will answer your prayer." ". . .no, no! I prayed but God never answered my prayers. He answered the prayers of other people, but not mine." "Witness, share your faith." ". . .Uh! Other people can lead them to Christ. I just can't do it."

We have to believe in God's promise, although we do not fully understand it. If we put our faith in it, God will bless us. Verse twenty-one says:

> and being fully assured that what He had promised, He was able also to perform.

"He was also able to perform" is the key for faith. You say, "Oh yes, I believe every promise in God's Word. Yes, I do! But it works for other people and not for me." Then, in reality, our God to you is a weak God, because you do not really believe that He is able to do it. He says, "I'll answer your

142

prayer," but you really do not believe that God has enough power to answer your particular prayer. You do not really believe that if He says He is going to do something, He can do it.

c. Assurance of God's power—He will There is another problem with Christians. They believe that God has said it, and maybe they believe that God can do it, but they do not think that He will do it. "I know God has said that He will answer my prayer, and that He will be with me when I witness. I know He can do it. But I just do not think that He will do it in my life. " That is where our faith fails. The Bible says in Matthew 6:33:

> But seek first His kingdom and His righteousness; and all
> these things shall be added to you.

We say that we believe in the promises of God. How is it then we worry so much? How come we spend so much time in our business, our work, our school, and we do not serve the Lord? Of course, we need to take care of those things, but the first thing is His Kingdom! God has promised power in our witnessing. How come we do not witness? "We don't think that God will give us the power." God has promised to forgive our sins when we confess them. "I know He has said that. I know He can forgive. But in my particular case, He will not do it." That is where our faith fails. If He says He will do it, He will do it in our lives. Why are we still feeling so guilty? Why are we harboring that sin? God will forgive if we confess. Oh, we know the promises of God, but we have such little faith.

The Destruction from Little Faith

Do you know what little faith is? Let us look at some of the characteristics of little faith. When we have little faith, we do not believe that God is going to do it. Do you remember the story of the man who fell off the cliff? He caught himself on a branch that was sticking out of the cliff. He cried, "Is anybody up there? Help me!" Then God answered, "I'm here. I'll help you." The man said, "Who are you?" "I'm God." "Can you help me, God?" God said, "I'll help you, but first, you must let go of the branch." The man thought and contemplated, and then he cried out, "Is anybody else up there?" Are we not just like that? If God promises something, He will do it. But we just will not let go of our own ideas.

Makes you worry Matthew 6:30 says:

> But if God so arrays the grass of the field, which is alive today and tomorrow is thrown into the furnace, will He not much more do so for you, O men of little faith?

Little faith makes you worry. You do not believe that God will provide for you and you begin to question. "Am I really saved? Does God really love me? Am I really going to heaven?" There are so many worries and so little faith.

Little faith brings out what we call the "what if" syndrome. "What if God is not really there?" "What if I fail my examination and cannot graduate?" "What if my business does not make money?" "What if I do not get married?" "What if I do get married?" There are so many questions, so many worries and so little faith.

Makes you fear Matthew 8:26 says:

> And He said to them, "Why are you timid, you men of little faith?" Then He arose, and rebuked the winds and the sea; and it became perfectly calm.

When the disciples were in a boat, a storm came. They were afraid. That is what little faith will do: It will bring fear to us. Men of little faith are always afraid of things. They become very pessimistic. Something good has happened. "That is

144

only an omen that something bad is going to come." Today is a beautiful day. "Ah, that means tomorrow is going to be a bad day." A man of little faith not only is afraid but also becomes superstitious. Therefore, there is no freedom in Christ and there is no joy in Christian life.

Makes you lose power   In Matthew 14:31, Peter was walking on the water. In verse twenty-nine, Peter actually walked on the water and he was the only other man in the world ever to walk on water, even for a short time. But then he began looking around him, he became afraid and began to sink. Verse thirty-one says:

> And immediately Jesus stretched out His hand and took hold of him, and said to him, "O you of little faith, why did you doubt?"

Little faith will cause you to doubt and lose power. Peter was walking on that water, because for a moment there, he had faith. But then, he began to doubt and he lost the power. When was the last time you were a man of faith? In the early part of your Christian life, when you were in the Word of God, you were praying, you were witnessing to everybody and you had faith that God was with you. But then you began to have doubt and you lost your power.

Makes you ignorant   Matthew 16:8 says:

> But Jesus, aware of this, said, "You men of little faith, why do you discuss among yourselves that you have no bread?"

Jesus was telling his disciples about the leaven of the Pharisees. They thought that Jesus was talking literally about bread, but Jesus was not talking about bread. He was talking about spiritual truth: The leaven is the sin and wickedness of the Pharisees. As the leaven permeates the dough of the bread, the sin and wickedness of the Pharisees also permeated the Church. Little faith will cause a lack of spiritual knowledge and perception.

Little faith will make you worry, make you fear, make you lose power and bring you a little way only. We need big faith. Big faith will bring us a long way to have assurance not only in God's promise but also in God's power; to believe that not only God can do what He promised us but also He will do it; and, to be able to believe not only in the facts but also in the Person.

The Development of Big Faith

How do we get big faith? I had little faith for five years. Certainly my faith has grown, and I want it to grow more. But for five years, I had "what if this?" and "what if that?" in my heart. I tried to be good but I always failed. Certain things that happened in my life have revolutionized my faith. I want to share that with you: I believe in God's Word.

The great chapter of faith in Hebrews, chapter eleven, is built upon Hebrews chapter ten. A person has to do what is in chapter ten before he can be in the Hall of Faith, with all those men of faith in chapter eleven.

Enter into God's presence Hebrews 10:19 says:

> Since therefore, brethren, we have confidence to enter the
> holy place by the blood of Jesus . . . .

That is the first thing for developing faith. We must enter the holy place. The holy place is the presence of God. We must enter into the presence of God.

We have come today and we have entered the church. But many here who have entered the church have not entered into the presence of God. Many of you have sung the good hymns, prayed along with our prayers and followed along the program of the worship service, but have not entered into the presence of God. You may have a time of Bible reading and prayer at home, but you have yet to enter into the presence of God. Your faith will never grow unless you really enter into and are totally immersed in the presence of God.

a. A quiet time You are so busy and you are so active in so many things, but God is not to be found in "busyness" or activity. God is to be found in quiet times. The Bible says:

Cease striving and know that I am God; (Ps. 46:10)

I like the New American Standard translation where it says, "Cease striving and know that I am God." A paraphrase would be "Will you stop what you are doing and know that I am God." We have many church activities, but we might have yet to enter into the presence of God. To be in the presence of God is to know Him, to acknowledge that He is here, to have a conversation with Him, to listen to Him and to have communion and fellowship with Him. It is not hard to do.

b. A prepared heart The Bible tells us that Jesus has provided the way—His blood was shed, so that you and I can enter into His presence. It is a new and a living way. You cannot come by the old way: Not by just trying to be good, nor by just coming to church. It has to be a living way, not a dead way. You have to come with a vitality in your heart, in total preparation to meet your God. What attitude do you have when you approach the living God?

Can you imagine what your reaction is when you see God? There ought to be fear and trembling in your heart, and at the same time, there is the boldness which the Lord has provided. Being totally in the presence of God would bring me to my knees. My heart would be pumping and there would be a shroud of fear in my heart, as well as sweetness and love for my God, my Creator. When I sing praises, it is going to be out of the joy in my heart. It does not have to be loud, but the joy and love is there. Have you ever entered into the presence of God? I know you had times like that before, but it has been a long time. That is why your faith is so little.

Exercise God's provision If you are going to come into the presence of God, you have to confess your sins. It says in Hebrews 10:22 that we:

> draw near with a sincere heart in full assurance of faith,
> having our hearts sprinkled clean from an evil conscience
> and our bodies washed with pure water.

God has provided the opportunity for faith in your life. But you need to exercise it. At the time of your birth, you already have all the muscles. The muscles have to be exercised and toned up, so that you can co-ordinate them. The Lord has provided the way to come to Him. Exercise it! How do you exercise it? Come to God! Draw near to Him! Approach Him! To do that, you must confess your sins and spend time with Him. You cannot enter into the presence of God when you are only giving five minutes. There must be a priority in your life.

"Oh, I want to be in the presence of God. I know that I'm in church but I'm not in the presence of God yet." So, quiet your heart, ready your self, confess your sins, and have your body "washed with pure water" (v. 22). If you want to increase your faith and exercise it, get baptized. God gives you the opportunity to pray. Pray! and your faith will grow. Come to prayer meeting! Last night we were at the Westminster Branch's fourth anniversary banquet. Dr. Lum said that they had 86 members and 90% of them came to prayer meeting. We have about 700 members in our mother church. We ought to see 600 in prayer meeting. Why are you not in prayer meeting? Do you not want your faith to grow? May God help us in this area.

Edify God's people   It says in verse twenty-four:

> and let us consider how to stimulate one another to love and
> good deeds . . . .

If you want your faith to grow, you have to be in fellowship.
The Bible says, "to consider." We have to think, to plan and to
find ways to stimulate one another to love and do good deeds.
"How can I make somebody love another person?" "How can
I make you love one another?" Such consideration will
encourage our faith. Exercise your faith! Do your best for the
Lord! You might fail. There are a lot of people who are
failing. A lot of people here feel that they have failed. Because
of that, their faith is also failing. God calls us to consider one
another—consider how we might stimulate one another to love
and do good deeds. We need to build up one another.

When we try to think of programs, try to think of ways
that can get people to love one another. Our moderator here
wants us to shake hands. At least that is something we can do.
When you leave this place, we want you to shake hands and
greet one another, and to sit down and talk to each other. We
need more fellowship. We have many fellowship meetings,
but we do not have fellowship. I said "fellowship," not
"fellowship meetings"! These meetings are supposed to
provide opportunities that fellowship will take place. It is
going to take place only when we are stimulating, provoking
and making each other love one another.

Brothers, you need to stimulate your sisters to love and do
good work! Wives, you have to encourage and stimulate your
husbands to love God and do good works. There are too many
husbands who are discouraging their wives from serving the
Lord and doing good works. The Bible tells us in verse
twenty-five that we ought to encourage one another, because
the day is drawing near. Then, the following verses talk about

backsliding. If we do not do this, we are backsliding, because our faith needs to be built up by one another. The day is drawing near; Jesus Christ is coming on that day. If we have faith, faith will produce faithfulness, which is exactly what He is going to judge us for when He comes again.

Are you a good and faithful servant? You will never be unless you have faith. If you only have a little faith, you will never be faithful. We must enter into His presence. I want to lead our congregation to enter into the presence of God. I want to lead you there, so you will be able to enjoy and relish the presence of God. Come to His presence and stay awhile, that your faith will grow. I want you to be there and I want to lead you there.

HOW TO LOVE GOD

The Importance of Loving God

Years ago, the great pioneer missionary Hudson Taylor was interviewing several candidates for the foreign missions field. He asked them the question, "Why do you want to be a foreign missionary?" One young man gave the answer, "Because of the Great Commission. The Lord commanded us to go out and preach the gospel." Another man answered, "Because there are millions of souls who are dying without knowing the name of Jesus." Others gave similar answers, but Hudson Taylor was not satisfied. He said, "All your answers are good, but I am afraid that they will fail you when you face severe testing and trial. There is only one true motive you must have if you are going to be successful as a missionary, and that motive is found in 2 Corinthians 5:14:

> For the love of Christ controls us, having concluded this,
> that one died for all, therefore all died . . . .

This verse should be true for every Christian. Whatever we are doing, the love of Christ must control our lives.

This word "control," in its Greek original, is found in other passages in the Bible. It is translated as "it grips you," "it seizes you," "you are pressed upon," "you are hemmed in" or "you feel trapped." Such are the effects of the love of Christ. It hems me in, it presses upon me, it grips me and it seizes my soul. There is no escape: I am trapped by the love of Christ. I am compelled to do what I do because of the love of Christ.

This is the only motivation every Christian needs to have. You may be serving the Lord; you may be doing terrific things; you may be very popular with people; and you may be very talented in many areas. But the Bible says that if you do not have love, you are nothing! Oh, we need to pay careful attention! Otherwise, we are just spinning our wheels, going nowhere. When we face the Lord, even though we say, "We did all these things, Lord," He will say, "You are nothing, for My love did not control you." Do you have love? You need to love God.

The command of God   In Mark 12:28, one of the scribes asked Jesus a question, "What commandment is the foremost of all?" Mark recorded the response in verse thirty:

> And you shall love the Lord your God with all your heart,
> and with all your soul, and with all your mind, and with all
> your strength.

You know, I thought that I was doing pretty well as a Christian: "I'm serving the Lord. I'm doing things for the Lord. If I think of any sins, I confess them right away. I feel pretty good in the Lord. . . ." Then I came across this commandment, the number one commandment—to love God with everything I have and everything I am.

Do you love God like that? If you do not love God like

that, you are in sin. This is the commandment, the number one commandment. You are to love God with all your heart, all your soul, all your mind and all your strength. That is to love Him with everything you have.

The scribe in this passage understood this. He told the Lord in verses thirty-two and thirty-three, "Right, Teacher, You have truly stated." Then he quoted the commandment and added that the commandment "is much more than all burnt offerings and sacrifices." Jesus saw that he answered intelligently, and He said to him, "You are not far from the Kingdom of God." Maybe you and I also know what this means. Maybe we too are not far from the Kingdom of God. But we are not there yet. We have to put this commandment into action. It is not good enough to KNOW the commandment; we have to DO it. Otherwise, we are not going to be in the Kingdom. You may not feel like it or circumstances may not allow it, but you must do it regardless. You are to love God. If you do not love God, then you will not be in the Kingdom of God.

The completion of God's love   Another reason for loving God is found in 1 John 4:12:

> No one has beheld God at any time; if we love one another,
> God abides in us, and His love is perfected in us.

No one has seen God, but when we have true love, God is there. Many people have not seen God and they have not even sensed that God is there. But, when love is there, they will sense God. So it is important for us to love one another. If we do not do that, people will not sense God. The last phrase, "His love is perfected in us," is not a clear translation from the Greek. God's love is already perfect; He does not need us to make it perfect. What this means is that God has set a goal for His love to touch every heart. When we love one another,

God can reach His goal for His love. When we are not loving one another, God's love cannot reach its goal. Therefore, if people's lives are not being touched, it is really your fault and mine, not God's. God's love wants to reach its goal, so let us love one another. That is important to loving God.

The confidence in God's judgment 1 John 4:17 is another important reason for loving God:

> By this, love is perfected with us, that we may have confidence in the day of judgment . . .

Are you afraid of the Day of Judgment? Many are afraid that Jesus is coming again. They are afraid to face the Lord. Yet, the Bible says in verse eighteen, "There is no fear in love." If you have fear, that means you do not love Him. If you love someone, you cannot wait to see him. You just long to see him. If you love the Lord, you will be looking forward to His appearance.

Love is a kind of a power that helps to purify us. Once, I read of a seventy-eight-year-old woman who had been smoking for fifty years. For those fifty years she tried to get rid of her smoking habit without success. She knew that it was a bad habit, but she just could not get rid of it. But then she met a seventy-nine-year-old man. This elderly man proposed marriage to her, upon the condition that she would give up her smoking. Immediately she gave it up, and she gave the reason why. She said, "For fifty years, I tried to give up smoking by my will power, but I couldn't do so until love came. That's what got rid of it."

If you love the Lord, you will want to straighten out your life. If you love the Lord, you do not want to hurt Him, so you will not sin. But many of you do not love the Lord. You are in sin, and that is why you are afraid of His coming. If you really have love for the Lord, you have the power to get rid of any bad habits of sin. Oh, why do you not have more confidence? Love the Lord, and do not be afraid. There is nothing to be afraid of. But instead, what great joy there will be on that Day of Judgment! Do not think that judgment is always to punish you. Judgment is also for good things. It is a time to reward Christians. So if you are right with the Lord, there is nothing to be afraid of. You will long for that Day. We need to love God and to know His love.

The Identification of Loving God

Description of God's love   Some of us do not know what love is. Love is not mushy infatuation or puppy love, where a girl bats her eyelashes and just "loves" the boy. Love is more serious than that.

a. The great example   We know about love from God. John 3:16 tells us that "God so loved the world." How do we know that God loved the world? We know because He gave us His only begotten Son, the One who is of the greatest value to Him. He gave Him to you and to me. Because of that, we know that love is giving and love is sacrificing. This is a clear demonstration of love. God did not shout down to the world, "World, I love you!" Instead, He demonstrated His love and did something. Love needs action.

b. The love chapter   If you look at the famous love chapter, 1 Corinthians chapter thirteen, you will find more descriptions about love. At the beginning of the chapter, it says that if you do all these things—speak in tongues, prophesy, know all mysteries and all knowledge and have all faith—but if you have no love, you are nothing. Then it continues from verse four saying that:

• "Love is patient, love is kind, and is not jealous." If

155

you are jealous or possessive about someone, that person is not truly your boy friend or girl friend, because you do not have genuine love.

• "Love does not brag and is not arrogant, does not act unbecomingly." Love never boasts of itself. Love loves without drawing attention. It does not want anybody to notice it. It just loves. Do you love like that?

• "Love does not seek its own." It just gives and does not seek for its own good. Love gives everything. It is more blessed to give than to receive.

• "Love is not provoked, does not take into account a wrong suffered." If somebody hurts you, you do not hold a grudge, you are not bitter, you do not hate and you are not angry—that is true love.

• "Love does not rejoice in unrighteousness, but rejoices with the truth." You and I might grab someone and say, "You heard what John did?" Then we might tell that person all the terrible things about John. We just love to tell the bad things about John. But that is not love. Love does not do that. It does not rejoice in unrighteousness. If John did something bad, you and I should be crying about it. Love rejoices in the truth. If John did something good, oh, we would want to tell everybody what John did. It seems that when we talk about other people, we always talk of the bad things about them. If that is what we do, we do not have love. We are seeking to boast about ourselves and cut other people down.

• "Love bears all things, believes all things, hopes all things, endures all things. Love never fails." Is that the kind of love you have? Love never gives up. People hurt you and people disappoint you, but you still love them. You do not give up.

c. The real love There are so many things about love. Let me give you three things to describe love and summarize all that I have said. This is very helpful for measuring your own love:

1. Love gives everything. It does not hold back.
2. Love does something. It takes action.
3. Love expects nothing. It just gives and does not expect anything in return.

Apply these three things to your love life—to your boy friend or girl friend, or just your good friend. If you are married, check it with your marriage partner. Do you love like that? You just give everything: "Whatever I have belongs to you, because you're my brother or sister in Christ."

This kind of love was made so evident to me one day. One day, I had to go to our mission, and my car was not working right. A brother found out and immediately said, "Here're the keys to my car. Take it. My car is your car." Oh, that is so good. Love gives everything. Love does something. Love expects nothing in return. Is that what you do when you love your marriage partner? Or do you do something and expect that "he better be doing something for me in return." If that is you, you do not have love.

Demonstration of God's love   For us to understand more about love, we need to know the first love. We have the very famous verse, 1 John 4:19:

> We love, because He first loved us.

If you and I do not understand about God's love, then we cannot love. If we do not have a relationship with God first, it is difficult for us to have true love. How do we know that God loved us first? Romans 5:8 says:

> But God demonstrates His own love toward us, in that while we were yet sinners, Christ died for us.

This is a clear demonstration of God's love. As verse seven says:

157

> For one will hardly die for a righteous man; though perhaps
> for the good man someone would dare even to die.

Do you know someone who would die for you? Do you have a friend or a loved one who would die for you? If a truck is out of control and is heading straight towards you, do you have a friend or a loved one who would push you away and be hit by the truck to save your life? How many of you would say, "Yes, I have at least one person who would do that for me?" Well, maybe you can think of one who would die for you, because you are his friend. That is why Romans 5:8 begins with the word, "But." What God has done is different from that situation. Your friend would die for you, because you are a friend. But God sent His Son to die for us when we were His enemies! Even though we were sinners, Christ died for us.

It saddens my heart that so many are indifferent and unmoved by the love of God through Christ. Many do not realize what Jesus has gone through for you and for me. As they betrayed Him, as they nailed Him to the cross, and as all the blood was gushing out of His veins, He could have called ten thousand angels. Oh, the excruciating pain! Yet He cried out, "Father, forgive them; for they do not know what they are doing" (Lk. 23:34). What we were doing was spitting on His face and slapping Him. Yet, He would still do it for us. He loves us. He first loved us. But, we did not love Him and we hated Him. As people, we cried along with the other people, "Crucify Him!" That is: "Get rid of Him," " I don't need Him," "I don't want him in my life" and "I could do very well without Him." Yet He would still die for you. Oh, how could you be unmoved?

The Bible says that Jesus loved the disciples to the end. Maybe you feel that you are at the end. You are about ready to give up; you just want to quit; you cannot take it anymore. But

Jesus loves you to the end. That is found in John chapter thirteen, where it says that Jesus loved them to the end. How did Jesus love them to the end? He took a towel and a basin of water, and He washed their feet. The Lord Jesus would stoop so low to get your love. He is even willing to wash your feet.

Discipline of God's love We see another form of His first love towards us. He cares about us so much. Even when we are wrong, He still loves us. We find this in Revelation 3:19:

> Those whom I love, I reprove and discipline; be zealous therefore, and repent.

The Lord knows when we are in sin, so He reproves and disciplines. But when God's discipline comes upon us, it is because He loves us. He wants us to be right with Him. Therefore we need to respond to His discipline. His Word disciplines us; His Holy Spirit convicts our hearts. We need to respond. How do we respond? "Be zealous therefore, and repent." What kind of sin are we in?

Look at the context of Revelation 3:15. The Lord Jesus says:

> I know your deeds . . . .

The Lord knows our deeds. We cannot escape the Lord. He knows all the wrong things we have done. He knows the right things we have done also. In speaking to the Laodicean Church, Jesus said:

> I know your deeds, that you are neither cold nor hot; I would that you were cold or hot. So because you are lukewarm, and neither hot nor cold, I will spit you out of My mouth. (Rev. 3:15-16)

These people were lukewarm. They were not hot and they were not cold. And such is the situation with many of us.

The Lord says, "I will spit you out of My mouth." In the

original language it is even stronger than that. Literally it means, "I will VOMIT you out of My mouth." You make the Lord sick! You are lukewarm. You have one foot in the world and one foot in the Church. You want to keep one foot in the world to be free to do all the sinful things there. At the same time, you will not give up the Church; you still want God in your life. You make the Lord sick! He will vomit you out of His mouth. Quit being lukewarm! And if you will not quit, then He would rather you be cold. Why do you not tear the Bible up, toss it in the fire, quit coming to church, curse God and forget it? The Lord would rather you be cold, than to be the way you are, "lukewarm."

In verse seventeen, these people are saying, "Oh, I am rich, and I have become wealthy, and have need of nothing." But the Lord says:

> you do not know that you are wretched and miserable and poor and blind and naked . . . .

Your life is shameful before God. No wonder you are afraid to face the Lord. You are lukewarm. But the Lord still loves you. He does not want you to stay in that state. So He tells you, "be zealous therefore, and repent." You better repent and commit your life to the Lord. Get rid of the self-sufficiency. We always need the Lord.

If you are an old-timer in the church and you think you know everything, if you think that you do not really need to be serious about the Lord, and if you think that you are doing pretty well in the world and you have no need, truly you do not know. May God open your eyes, and let you see that you are lukewarm. You make the Lord sick, and He will vomit you out. Oh, brothers and sisters, repent, confess your sins and get right with God. It is not worth it otherwise.

The Implementation of Loving God

I know that many of you do love God. You know He first loved you, and you really want to love Him. But some of us do not know how to love Him. "I can't see God." "I love God so much, but I can't hug Him." "I can't kiss God. I can't shake His hand. I can't because He is not physical." It does not seem to be enough just to say, "God, I love you." Since He loves us so much, we want to do something for Him. How can we love Him back? Well, the Bible tells us many ways.

Keep His commandments Let us look at John chapter fourteen. This is how we can love Him. John 14:15 is a very simple but profound statement:

> If you love Me, you will keep My commandments.

Verse twenty-one says:

> He who has My commandments and keeps them, he it is who loves Me . . . .

And verse twenty-three says:

> Jesus answered and said to him, "If anyone loves Me, he will keep My word . . . ."

If you really love the Lord, you will obey His commandments, you will keep them, you will do them and you will maintain them.

You say, "How can I keep the commandments? I don't even know what they are." Oh yes, you do! In this passage, it tells us that there is the Holy Spirit, the Helper who will bring all things to our remembrance. He will guide us to all truth. Right now the Holy Spirit is showing each one of you in your own heart some of the commandments. You know the Ten Commandments. You know that you should be baptized. You know that you should pray. You know that you should read the Bible. You know that you should attend church faithfully. You know that you should give tithes and offerings. These are very clear. And the Holy Spirit tells you. Do not play dumb. If you are a true Christian, you know the commandments and you have the responsibilities. Keep His commandments through obedience. Do you love the Lord? Then, obey His commandments. Are you faithful in keeping these commandments? The Holy Spirit is showing many of you right now that you are not keeping some of these commandments. That means you do not love Him. If you love Him, you will do it. Let the Holy Spirit speak to your heart.

Persevere under trials Here is another way to love God. James 1:12 is a tremendous verse:

> Blessed is a man who perseveres under trial; for once he has been approved, he will receive the crown of life, which the Lord has promised to those who love Him.

How wonderful is the crown of life which the Lord is going to give to those whom He has promised—the ones who love Him! If you love the Lord, you are going to get a crown. If you love the Lord, you will enter into His Kingdom. That is why it is so important to have love. If you do not love God, you will not enter His Kingdom. It is for those who love Him, for those who persevere under trial and meet the approval of God. You have to keep on persevering and enduring under trials. In spite of all the storms of life, you wait on the Lord. That means you love Him, and you do not quit. God would never give you and me anything more than we can take. He is trying to stretch us so that we can be ready for His coming. These trials and sufferings are only momentary. Do not give up! You have to hold fast. You are right at the threshold of deliverance. The answer is coming soon. You have to hold on.

I remember hearing stories about women who were about to give birth. There was one particular woman who was in the last stage of labor, which is usually the most painful stage. Many times when women are in such pain, they begin to say things they really do not mean. This particular woman was in such great pain at this time that she was going to give up. She said, "I can't take it anymore!" She began getting out of bed and said, "I'm getting out of here!" And the poor husband patted her hand and said, "Oh dear, it's okay, just hold on." And she took her hand away and said, "Don't touch me! It's all your fault!" Then the baby was delivered and there was great joy and smiles, for deliverance had come and the pain was gone. Some of you are in pain now. Maybe you are blaming other people. But you are at the threshold of deliverance! Do not give up. Persevere! If you love God, God has a crown for you. He has promised.

Love one another   Finally, we have another way to love God in 1 John 4:20-21. God loves you so much and you want to love Him back, but how? One way is to keep His commandments. Another way is to persevere under trials. And there is a third way. It says in 1 John 4:20:

> If someone says, "I love God," and hates his brother, he is a liar . . . .

Verses twenty and twenty-one tell us that if you love God, you will love your brother. When you shake your brother's hand, you are shaking the hand of God. When you give your brother or sister a hug, you are giving God a hug. When you give a cup of cold water to the least of these, you have done it unto the Lord. Do you want to love God? Love one another.

How do we love one another? There are many verses that

tell us the way and here is one. Galatians 5:13 says:

> For you were called to freedom, brethren; only do not turn your freedom into an opportunity for the flesh, but through love serve one another.

"Through love serve one another." In the original language this word "serve" means "to serve as a slave." It says in this verse that you have freedom. Use your freedom to make yourself a slave. Through love, serve as a slave to one another. If all of you consider your brothers and sisters as your masters, then everybody will be a slave to one another. Oh, that will really be something!

I remember years ago at camp, we had an interesting experience. We had what was called a "leg auction" to raise money for camperships. They gathered a lot of people together, and wrapped a sheet all the way around them. No one could see who they were. Everybody under the sheet rolled up their pants, so all that could be seen were legs. There were fat legs, skinny legs, hairy legs, smooth legs and all kinds of legs. During the auction, each person behind the sheet would dance around and try to attract people to buy their legs. After someone bought the pair of legs, they would reveal to whom the legs belonged and that person became "a slave" to the buyer at camp. He would serve the "master" dinner and do all kinds of things for him. And we laughed and had all kinds of fun.

That is exactly what happens with Christians. When we serve one another with love, it should be fun, lots of fun and laughter! It is a great joy to be a slave to one another, for it is more blessed to give than to receive.

So many of you have already shown yourselves to be slaves to my wife, Annie, and to me: All your flowers, cards, phone calls, prayers, food—oh, so much food. We appreciate it very much. One brother really stands out in my mind. That time when my wife was in the hospital and my kids were in different homes, I was ministering in camp. This brother got hold of our house keys. He went into our house, mopped the floor, vacuumed the carpet and did all kinds of housecleaning. Nobody knew. This brother was out of a job at that time, so he took it upon himself to be a slave to our household. I was really blessed. Another brother was willing to take a day off from work to take Annie to the hospital. Oh, what great love! How wonderful if we could show this kind of love to one another.

There are three elements to being a slave:
1. You need to support one another,
2. You need to serve one another, and
3. You need to surprise one another.

Keep the element of surprise in there. Do things for people when they least expect it. Maybe it is a letter you send anonymously in the mail to encourage a person, to support him and to let him know that you love him. Or, maybe you know somebody who needs financial help. Send him some money anonymously. You may not have much money, but give him something along with a little note to encourage him. And do not tell anybody. As soon as you tell somebody, it is no longer love, because love expects nothing in return. As soon as you tell somebody else, you expect someone to praise you, "Look what I did." Just do not tell anybody; keep it only between you and God. You support, you serve and you surprise! We need to express our love to one another. Let someone know that he belongs. Let someone know that you are glad that he is there, with a smile, a hand shake or a hug. And God will bless.

Brothers and sisters, let us love God. Check your love. Does it give everything? Does it do anything? Does it expect nothing in return? If you love God, God will bless you. To love God is to keep His commandments, to persevere under trials and to love one another. We can love one another by supporting one another, serving one another and surprising one another. The church will grow, because without love we are nothing!

TO BE GREAT IN GOD'S KINGDOM

The question every dedicated Christian would have is, "Can this be the year our Lord Jesus will come again?" It is very clear that things in this world are getting worse, not getting better, and this is in accordance with the prophecy found in the Scripture. Now is the end time. Can this be the year Jesus Christ will come again?

I do not know where you are in your thinking. Maybe you have not thought about the seriousness of Jesus Christ in your life. But you know, it does not matter what you believe or what I believe, because truth is truth. When something is true, it will happen no matter what we believe. So our responsibility is to discover the truth. If Jesus Christ is really coming again soon, maybe this year, we better change our lives. His coming soon better have some effect on our lives. If you do not believe in God or Jesus Christ, I encourage you to investigate the truth, for we Christians believe that Jesus is coming again and that He will establish His Kingdom. If you are a Christian today, your purpose is to prepare and be trained for that time.

The Desire

The goal of a Christian is to reign with Christ in His Kingdom. God has called us to be great in His Kingdom, and this is His will for all Christians. Let us have a clear understanding that for us to be great in His Kingdom is not for our own benefit, but God wants us to be great in His Kingdom because He is a great God. Who are we? How can it be possible that God taking this lump of clay and making it great in the Kingdom will give greatness to Him? There is nothing we can do to make ourselves great in God's eyes. But if God would make us great in His Kingdom, it would give glory to Him and show that our God is a great God.

Is it your desire to be great in God's Kingdom? I know it is true that many Christians do not even care, because there has not been enough enlightenment. We need to pray that God will open our eyes to this desire He has upon us. You might say, "I'm nothing. I can't do anything." But you are the one God wants to make great, so that all the glory will be His, and not yours.

Since the creation   This has been God's desire ever since the beginning. Please turn to Genesis 1:26 for the great pronouncement: "Let Us make man in Our image." It is amazing that God would want to make something out of the dust of the ground and want this "something"—Man— to be in His image (that alone is already greatness), and that He would let Man rule. God created Man so that Man could rule, and a ruler is great. In verse twenty-eight, He told the man and the woman:

> Be fruitful and multiply, and fill the earth, and subdue it;
> and rule . . . .

That is why we have this inherent trait in our nature: the desire to achieve and to be successful. The word "subdue" means to gain mastery over. Ever since the beginning, Man has wanted to be the master of his world. So, there comes the motivation to do research, experimentation and discovery. To be great and gain mastery over the world is good, and is a God-given desire. God's original purpose was for Man to gain mastery, to rule and to be great.

Since the resurrection But sin entered into the world and Man fell. Then we see a distortion in Man's desire. No longer is it to be great under God's direction but for selfish gains. Cain wanted his sacrifice to be better than Abel's. But because his sacrifice was not acceptable to God, he killed his brother. Evil multiplied, and thus, the flood came as judgment. We see it in the Tower of Babel, when the people of the earth tried to build a tower to reach God and be greater than God. We see the splendor of the kingdom of Israel under Solomon's rule. And then when Solomon's son Rehoboam boasted that he would be greater than his father, the kingdom was split into two.

Throughout the Bible and throughout human history, Man has tried to achieve greatness, but it has been a sinful type of greatness. Praise the Lord that our God loves us, and His desire upon us still is to be great in His Kingdom. So, He sent His Son, Jesus Christ. The angel Gabriel visited Mary, told her that she would be with child, and pronounced that the child "will be great." Jesus lived and died. He died for our sins—to take away our sinful nature—that we can return according to God's way of greatness. Jesus Himself was exalted. The Bible says, "every knee should bow. . .every tongue should confess that Jesus Christ is Lord" (Phil. 2:10-11). Christ's ascension to the Father gives us the way to greatness. Many times we talk about the death and the resurrection of our Lord, but have we ever considered the practical significance of the ascension of our Lord?

a. A dwelling place Take a look with me and turn to John 14:2:

> In My Father's house are many dwelling places; if it were not so, I would have told you; for I go to prepare a place for you.

The Lord blessed me with this verse recently. Jesus is speaking about a beautiful place in heaven, and then He says, "if it were not so, I would have told you." I thank the Lord because I have not heard a word from the Lord. The Lord has never told me otherwise. If it were not so, He would have told me! I thank the Lord because he has not told me, and therefore, I know it is true. There are many dwelling places, and the Lord is preparing one for me; this He could not do unless He ascended to the Father. So the first practical significance of the ascension of our Lord is that He can go and prepare a place for us.

b. A greater work In John 14:12, it says:

> Truly, truly, I say to you, he who believes in Me, the works that I do shall he do also; and greater works than these shall he do; because I go to the Father.

Here we see the second practical significance of the ascension. Because He went to the Father, He could provide us with the ability to do greater works. We cannot do works greater than those of Jesus in terms of quality, for nobody can match the works of Jesus in quality. But in terms of extent and quantity, Jesus Christ was limited to Palestine and there was a lesser population at that time. Today we have a bigger world: There are opportunities for travel, and there are more people in this world whom we can pray for. The extent of our work is so much greater; our giving capacity is much greater as well. The Lord has provided us with all these, because He went to the Father. In John 14:16 the Lord says that He will ask the Father and He will send us the Holy Spirit. So, how wonderful it is, because He went to the Father, He could send the Holy Spirit to give us the power we need.

c. A divine presence   But, Jesus says in John 14:18:

> I will not leave you as orphans; I will come to you.

It is a paradox for He says that He is going away, and now He says that He will come to us. And then later, He talks about how His Father and He will come and make abode in us. Because of His ascension, Jesus can make His spiritual presence to be with us. He is no longer limited in the body. How else can He say to us: "Lo, I am with you always" (Mt. 28:20)? Jesus can be with you and in you at this very moment.

d. A spiritual joy   Look at John 14:28:

> You heard that I said to you, "I go away, and I will come to you." If you loved Me, you would have rejoiced . . . .

His ascension is a source for our joy. Jesus is accepted by the Father; salvation for us is secured; there are dwellings for us; His power is available to us; and Jesus is able to come again. It is a source of joy. Praise the Lord for His ascension. We can do greater works.

The Way

Believe in Him   How can we do greater works? In John 14:12, He says, "he who believes in Me. . . ." To do greater works, we must believe in Him. If we do not believe in Jesus Christ, we cannot do anything, as He has said, "he who abides in Me, and I in him, . . .for apart from Me you can do nothing" (Jn. 15:5). So, first of all, believe in Him.

Do His works Secondly, He says, "the works that I do shall he do also" (Jn. 14:12). If you want to do greater works, then you must do the works of Christ. What are some of the things that Jesus did? Jesus prayed; you should pray. Jesus went to church to worship God, He read the Bible and He shared his faith. You and I should do the same. Believe in Him. Do His works.

Ask for His glory Thirdly, Jesus talks about prayer, "whatever you ask in My name, that will I do, that the Father may be glorified in the Son" (Jn. 14:13). Ask in prayer with the purpose to glorify God. Most of us pray for selfish gains. Many of us pray for our parents that they will come to know the Lord. Certainly, that is God's will, is it not? Sure, it is. But be careful. Our prayer might be that we want our parents to be saved so that we can feel better, and we can have the assurance of their going to heaven. We have forgotten that our prayer should be that they be saved, so that our God will be glorified, and God's name will be exalted. Jesus says here: "If you ask Me anything in My name, I will do it" (Jn. 14:14). But, it needs to be with the intention that God be glorified.

Will you check your prayers? Why do you ask for the things you ask for? Is it that God will be glorified, or is it more that you will feel better? Let us examine ourselves. If the Lord says it, believe it. Believe in the Lord. Do the works of the Lord. Ask in the name of the Lord. Then, you will be doing greater works, and you will be great in God's Kingdom.

Do not be discouraged Some people say, "I've tried to serve the Lord." Maybe they are discouraged. Many years ago there was a missionary named Rev. Morrison. He spent his whole life doing pioneer work as a missionary in China, and it came to the point where it was time for him to retire. This old man was taking a steamship home back to America. It just so happened that on the same steamship was President Theodore Roosevelt, coming back from a vacation. As the ship approached New York harbor, Rev. Morrison could see welcome signs and banners. A band was playing and millions of people were cheering. He knew that all the fanfare was for the President, and he began to feel sorry for himself. "No one will be meeting me at the dock. No one even cares what I did in China. I spent my whole life; who cares?" Rev. Morrison folded his hands and leaned against the railing of the ship. And as he did that, Rev. Morrison writes, suddenly he heard a voice like the sound of many waters. As he was wallowing in self-pity, the voice said to him, "But you are not home yet."

Brothers and sisters, do not be discouraged. Maybe you have a sense of failure in your past. Do you not know that there are new opportunities ahead? The Lord's desire upon you is to do greater works. God is looking forward that you will be great in His Kingdom. Maybe you do not see the fruits of your work now, but you are not home yet. Just wait until you get home, and then watch out for those banners, the music and the band.

The Detour

God's desire for us is to be great in His Kingdom. But being human as we are, it is so easy to get off the track. Let us see how it is possible to detour off the track God has for us.

Annul God's commandment Turn to Matthew 5:19. Here in the context of the great Sermon on the Mount, Jesus is speaking about the Kingdom:

> Whoever then annuls one of the least of these
> commandments, and so teaches others, shall be called least
> in the kingdom of heaven; but whoever keeps and teaches
> them, he shall be called great in the kingdom of the heaven.

It is very clear that some will be called "least" and others will
be called "great" in the Kingdom. The one who will be least is
the one who annuls one of the least of these commandments.
The verb "annuls" is of the same root as the verb "to abolish"
the Law in Matthew 5:17. "To abolish" is a stronger word, a
more intense word, while "to annul" is a milder form. "To
annul" a commandment means to set aside, to disregard and to
neglect the commandment. Here, it is not talking about the big
commandments, but the least of these commandments. It is not
the big commandment that is going to ruin our lives. "I have
not murdered anybody. I have not stolen that much money. I
have not told too many lies." It is not the big sin, but the little
disobedience that will ruin us.

Of course, we realize that before God, all commandments
are important. It is only in our thinking that some of these
commandments are lesser and some are greater. We are careful
not to murder anybody. We know that we should not lie, nor
cheat, nor steal. Maybe there are other areas like disobeying
our parents, a little cheating on income taxes, or cheating in
school. The one who annuls the least of these commandments
and so teaches others shall be called least in the Kingdom of
heaven. The Lord says, "Forgive one another." "But look at
what that guy did to me!" The Lord says, "Forgive him." "I
have forgiven him seven times already." The Lord says,
"Seventy times seven" (Mt. 18:22). When the Lord gives a
commandment, we are to obey, not to lay aside, annul or
disregard.

Doubt God's Son Another way we can detour from
God's will is found in Matthew 11:11. I have wrestled with

this passage. Jesus says:

> Truly, I say to you, among those born of women there has
> not arisen anyone greater than John the Baptist; yet he who
> is least in the kingdom of heaven is greater than he.

Yes, John the Baptist is a great one, but not greater than anyone in the Kingdom. Why did the Lord say this? Was John the Baptist not a man of God? Is he going to be the least of the least in the Kingdom of heaven? Or does it mean that he is not even going to be in the Kingdom of heaven?

Matthew 11:2-3 gives the reason why John is the least in God's Kingdom:

> Now when John in prison heard of the works of Christ, he
> sent word by his disciples, and said to Him, "Are You the
> Expected One, or shall we look for someone else?"

John had doubted Jesus. You remember that at the Jordan River when John was baptizing, he pronounced to the world that someone greater than he himself was coming. When Jesus arrived on the scene, he pronounced to the world that Jesus was the Messiah, the one he was waiting for. "Behold, the Lamb of God who takes away the sin of the world!" (Jn. 1:29). But now John was in prison. I tried to think as he thought; I might have done the same thing. "I am in prison. I am discouraged. I can hear the music upstairs where Herod is having a party. Pretty soon my head will be cut off. Before they put me in prison, I said, "All right, go ahead. Put me in prison. Jesus is here. You better watch out because He is going to do something." But Jesus has not done anything. I am still in prison. What's happening?"

You and I are like that. We believe in Jesus and believe that He is coming again. But, 2,000 years have gone by. "Is it really true?" Doubt easily creeps in. "Are You the Expected One, or shall I look elsewhere?" "Maybe I shouldn't give as much money to the church as I used to. Maybe I shouldn't spend so much time at church and in serving the Lord. After all, I only have one life to live; I think I ought to have some fun."

When doubt creeps in, you will no longer be great in God's Kingdom. You have given your life to Him in dedication, and now you try to take it back. You will lose what God intends for your life. That happened to Moses. He could not enter the promised land. He was the one who led the Israelites out of Egypt, but he could not enter in. That happened to Judas Iscariot. The close relationship he must have had with Jesus personally, yet he betrayed the Lord. Are you close to the Lord now? Do not lose what you have!

The Demand

Become a child How can we be great in God's Kingdom? In Matthew 18:1-2, the Bible says:

> At that time the disciples came to Jesus, saying, "Who then is greatest in the kingdom of heaven?" And He called a child to Himself . . . .

We know from the other gospel accounts that the disciples were arguing with each other. Peter said, "I am going to be the greatest in the Kingdom." But John said, "I am going to be greater than you." And then there was argument and dispute among all the disciples. Jesus even asked them in Mark's account: "What were you discussing on the way?" (Mk. 9:33). And they were afraid to tell Him. So finally, they asked the question, "Who then is the greatest in the Kingdom of heaven?" Jesus then called a child to Himself. How shocking it was to the disciples. In the world of Roman emperors, kings, pharisees and high priests, Jesus called a child. Jesus says in Matthew 18:3:

Truly I say to you, unless you are converted and become like children, you shall not enter the kingdom of heaven.

Here they were arguing who would be the greatest in the Kingdom, and Jesus said you might not even enter the Kingdom of heaven.

a. Be converted First of all, you must be converted. Conversion is not just being saved. Jesus was talking to His disciples who already believed in the Lord. He is talking to you and to me. We are already Christians. "To convert" means "to turn away." What are we to turn away from? The disciples were arguing. They had rivalry, ambition, envy and jealousy. God calls you and me to turn away from such things. Quit trying to be better than other people. Quit forming your little groups and excluding others. Turn away from such things; reach out like you ought to. Quit trying to show your pomp and pride. You better turn away from such things and become like little children.

b. Be humble What kind of child was this? Well, we know that Jesus called this child, so this child could respond to a call. In Luke's account, we see that this child could walk and he stood by Jesus (Lk. 9:47). Therefore, this child was not an infant or a baby. And in Mark's account, we see that Jesus took this child in his arms. This child could walk and could respond to a call, but was small enough so that Jesus could take him in His arms. The child was one or two years old; the child was a toddler. I challenge you sometimes to go down to our nursery, then you will know how humble children can be.

We have the wrong idea about humility. There was a pastor who came to a church by himself. He knelt down humbling himself and prayed to the Lord, "I am nothing. O Lord, I am nothing." Then the assistant pastor came in. When he saw the pastor, he got convicted, so he knelt down next to the pastor, humbled himself and said, "I am nothing. I am nothing." Then the youth director came by and saw the pastor and the assistant pastor kneeling and saying "I am nothing." He knelt by the assistant pastor and said, "I am nothing. I am nothing." The deacon saw the three of them there. He came and knelt down by the youth director and began to pray, "I am nothing. I am nothing." And the janitor came by and saw the four of them. And he came and knelt down by the deacon and began to pray, "I am nothing. I am nothing!" The deacon noticed the janitor kneeling down next to him. And he yelled to the youth director saying, "Hey, guess who thinks he's nothing!" There is a possibility of pride in our humility.

c. Be simple Humility is not just putting yourself down. Jesus shows us what humility is here: the pattern of a child. What is this pattern? The pattern is that of simplicity. A child is a simple person. When you call to a child, he will come to you. He is not very complex in his thinking. When you call, he will not say, "Well, I don't know whether I should come or not. Who are you?" When you give him a piece of candy, he will eat it with the wrapper and everything. A child is very simple. You and I are so complicated in our thinking. 2 Corinthians 11:3 says:

> But I am afraid, lest as the serpent deceived Eve by his craftiness, your minds should be led astray from the simplicity and purity of devotion to Christ.

God calls us to a simplicity and purity of devotion to Christ. Many of us have lost that simplicity. How is it with your devotion? It is to be simple before the Lord. Just say, "Lord, I love you." Just read the Bible as it is. You do not have to bring real deep complicated thoughts into the Bible at all, not questions like, "Who made God?" "Where did God come from?" He wants simplicity and purity of devotion. Just pray to the Lord; just believe the Bible as it is. Do not be so complicated and try to question, "Hey, there may be errors in the Bible!" Accept it, believe it and trust it as a child. That is a sign of greatness.

The one who humbles himself as a child is the greatest in the Kingdom. That is the problem with Bible professors, scholars and theologians. They study so much and they get into such deep thought in theology, that they lose the simplicity and purity of devotion before the Lord. Knowledge puffs up. Put the Bible first. We need to maintain a simple devotion before the Lord.

Become a slave The Lord calls us to slavery. If you want to be great in God's Kingdom, you will be a servant to all, a slave, to everyone. I used to imagine how nice it would be if I were on some tropical island, with these slaves around me, fanning me, feeding me with grapes and giving me all that I needed. The Bible calls us not only to be slaves in Christ but also, more concretely, to be slaves to one another. The Bible tells us to serve as slaves to one another through love (Gal. 5:13).

Have a slave's attitude towards one another, not a master's attitude. "What can I do for you?" When someone has a need, I will try to meet that need. Check yourself. Are you doing that? Are you reaching out to our visitors? "We're so happy you came. Is there anything we can do for you?"—a slave's attitude! I know many of you are doing that already, and many are blessed because of your work. Keep it up. Some of you have not seen the light yet. See to it this year. You might make some phone calls; or you might do visitation. Try to meet the needs of others.

Because I am indebted, I am a bond servant to other people. That is the mind of the one who will be great in God's Kingdom. God calls us to simplicity and He calls us to be slaves. If we do so, we will be great in God's Kingdom.

LET US NOT LOSE SIGHT
OF OUR PURPOSE

Our Purpose

The Commission of God The last words of our Lord Jesus Christ in the Gospel of Matthew before He left this world was to "make disciples" (Mt. 28:19). In the Gospel of Mark, the Lord said, "preach the gospel to all creation" (Mk. 16:15). In the Gospel of Luke, it was "You are witnesses" (Lk. 24:48). And in the Gospel of John, He commanded, "as the Father has sent Me, I also send you" (Jn. 20:21).

The purpose for us The Lord has given us a commission to carry out. He said this just before He left the world. If anyone is going to leave this world, his last words are very important. Thus, the Church of God was established primarily to make disciples for God's Kingdom, and this is true for our church here. We ought to be shaping up people, edifying, discipling and preparing them for God's Kingdom.

Everything we are doing as a Church is to be for this purpose. What we do as a Christian is to be for this purpose as well. We are not a social club or a social welfare agency or a fellowship group primarily. This is not a counselling center, not a political action group, not a Chinese school and not a day-care center. This is not just a nice place to meet other Chinese people. Our purpose is to make disciples for God's Kingdom.

Stifling Our Purpose

I am afraid that we are beginning to lose sight of that purpose. Where is the spirit of evangelism? Where are all the people we want to introduce to Jesus Christ? Why are we not seeing more people coming to the Lord? Do we care about missions? Do we have love for the lost souls? The great commission of our Lord is found in Matthew chapter twenty-eight, after the resurrection of our Lord. When we read Matthew chapter twenty-eight, we see that there were efforts made to conceal the truth of His resurrection. The resurrection is pivotal to our faith and message. It is amazing to see how the very same methods are used today to stifle the message of our God.

Bribery In Matthew 28:11, the soldiers who were guarding the tomb of Jesus came to the chief priests. In verse twelve, when they came together, the elders gave a large sum of money to the soldiers. They wanted the soldiers to hide the truth, so they bribed them. Jesus Christ rose from death and conquered death, and so shall everyone who puts his faith and trust in Jesus Christ. Satan knows that he cannot reverse the resurrection, but he can stop the message from going out. So he made the elders bribe the soldiers.

Satan is bribing Man today as well. There are so many distractions in this world. There is the love of money and riches. There is the American dream which is the dream of every man. Satan has bought many people, and they have lost the message of Jesus Christ. People are busier making money than serving the Lord. Do you know more about making money than making disciples? Do you know more about how to win in the stock market and in gambling than to win souls? Are you investing in riches of this world rather than laying up treasures in heaven?

They gave the soldiers a large sum of money—money that brought them away from witnessing what they saw. In Matthew 28:2, the soldiers felt an earthquake and the angel of the Lord came. In verse four, when they saw the angel, they shook with fear and fell down like dead men. They felt the earthquake and they saw the angel, but they were quieted by money. There are Christians today that are quieted in sharing the gospel. They have lost sight of the purpose of God. Satan bribed them, and they took the bait.

I was so impressed by our sister Eleanor Tang's sharing about Thailand. She showed pictures of how the Thai people gave all their wealth to build the Buddhist temples, the idols and the shrines. You have seen those huge edifices with spiralling towers built out of pure gold. Then, you look at the people. They are content to be farmers and hard laborers. They are willing to live a simple life style, so that all their gold and wealth can go to their temples and their gods. How much dedication do Christians have? Why can we not relegate ourselves to a simpler life style? Let the money and wealth we have be given to glorify God, that His message can go forth. Alas, we have been bribed and we bought it! We begin to lose sight of God's purpose for the Church.

Let us face it—we are losing the battle! When will we learn that money can buy a bed, but cannot buy sleep? Money can buy books but not a brain. Money can buy a house but not a home. Money can buy medicine but not health. Money can buy amusement but not happiness. Money can buy religion but not salvation. "You cannot serve God and mammon" (Mt. 6:24). God, help us to have a simpler life style! Why must we buy the most expensive and luxurious thing? Why do we have to buy the most expensive sports cars? We set our standards so high on money. Where do we put our God? As long as we are bribed by temporal things, we lose sight of the purpose of God.

Apology The elders told the soldiers in Mt. 28:13:

> You are to say, "His disciples came by night and stole Him away while we were asleep."

Do you know that soldiers who fell asleep on duty would be executed? This was a ridiculous explanation against the resurrection. This is an excuse of rationalization.

Many Christians today make apology for their faith. Did Jesus Christ rise from the dead? Did he or did he not give us the Great Commission? So what is our excuse? What apology are we making? Why is it so hard for us to share our faith? Some of us think that we cannot share our faith with other people, because it will become a burden to their lives if they know about Jesus. Some of us really do not believe that people need Jesus, thinking that, "They are living a pretty good life. They are good people. Why should I burden them with Jesus Christ?" Then you really do not believe that Jesus is the only way to God. And the purpose of God is stifled in your life, and it becomes stifled in the Church of God.

When will we learn that we are to be witnesses for the Lord wherever we are? We have to witness in our schools, our jobs, our families, as well as in our church. We are not to play a different role outside the church. We ought to be Christians wherever we are. Quit making excuses for being a Christian.

Let us get rid of the apologies. We ought to claim our jobs and our schools for Jesus Christ. Those are our fields of missions. We are to be His witnesses there.

Do you know what a witness means? What is a witness supposed to tell in court? He is supposed to tell what he saw, what he heard and what he experienced. That is exactly what you and I are to do. Just tell about Jesus. We have seen Him, we have heard of Him and we have experienced Him. That is all.

Security The elders said in verse fourteen:

> if this should come to the governor's ears, we will win him
> over and keep you out of trouble.

Nobody wants to get into trouble; nobody wants to make trouble. But, if that is your mind as a Christian, you will stifle the purpose of God in your life. You better know it, and you better know it right now. If you are to be a Christian and a witness for the Lord, you are going to make trouble. The Lord Jesus Himself said in Matthew 10:34:

> I did not come to bring peace, but a sword.

If we are going to be true Christians, we are going to encounter the world, which is the enemy of God. Anyone who makes friends with the world will be an enemy of God. We are going to make trouble. We are going to encounter embarrassment and ridicule.

It is not easy to be a Christian. Too many Christians today do not know how hard it is to be a Christian. Do not think that once you become a Christian, then all your troubles will go away. There are going to be more troubles if you really are going to be a committed Christian. There will be friction between you and the world. If you want to dwell in security and do not want to cause any trouble, then you will stifle the work of God. We are to move out for God. "Onward

Christian Soldiers!" It is not easy; it is embarrassing.

I remember years ago I had to share my faith with my father. He had a heart attack, but he came out of it. I knew that I had to talk with him about the Lord. How could I talk to my father about religion? However, the Lord convicted my heart. I might be embarrassed. He might ridicule me; he might cut me down because I went into the ministry. How do you talk to your father about God? But I had to! It was worth the embarrassment and it was worth the troubles. I did not care what was going to happen to me. I only wanted him to be saved. Praise God that he did pray with me to receive Jesus Christ. Are your father, your mother and your friends saved? If you do not want to talk to them about Jesus because you do not want to cause them trouble, you stifle the work of God! If you are going to be a true Christian, you will cause trouble.

Conformity   In Matthew 28:15, it tells us that the soldiers

> took the money and did as they had been instructed . . . .

Too many Christians have taken the bribe. They are doing exactly what Satan is instructing them, and they stifle the purpose of God. Verse fifteen continues:

> this story was widely spread among the Jews, and is to this day.

If people could see that it was a false story, then it would never have been widely spread. However, so many conformed to the story. I wonder if some of us have also listened to this or other concocted stories. "After all, no one else is sharing his faith. Why should I?" You have conformed to other people, and you have not done what God has sent you to do. You are stifling the work of God and losing sight of the purpose of the Church. God, help us that we will be delivered from this.

We have to break out from this mold, brothers and sisters.

We have been squeezed to conform to what a Church ought to be, but in reality, we have not been what a Church ought to be. We are living a pseudo–Christianity, not a true Christianity. We are not living a normal Christian life! Do you want to know what a normal Christian life is? Read the book of Acts, then you will find out what a normal Christian life ought to be. We conform too much to the world. Let us live a simpler life style. Let us love the Lord. Let us not love ourselves.

Strengthening Our Purpose

Keep our appointments with God   Praise the Lord that in verse sixteen it says:

> But the eleven disciples proceeded to Galilee, to the mountain which Jesus had designated.

The disciples went to the mountain. There is something special about the mountain. You and I need to go to a mountain and to get to the mountain top to meet the Lord. Well, we cannot go to the mountain everyday, can we? But, sometimes we ought to go. Some of you went to camp this past summer and you had a good time. We were on the mountain to meet the Lord. The Lord wants us to meet Him, not just on the mountain, but in the park or even in our own bedroom.

We need to keep appointments with the Lord, so that we can know the heart of God. If we spend time with the Lord in prayer and reading His Word, we will begin to know the heart of God. If we really know the heart of God, we will feel as God feels. The disciples walked miles to get to the mountain. Will you go and meet the Lord? Keep appointments with Him, whether it is in your personal devotional times or coming to church. Keep appointments with the Lord, and get to know the heart of God.

Cultivate our worship to God   Then it says, in verse seventeen:

And when they saw Him, they worshipped Him . . . .

They adored Him. They loved Him. Maybe, they were like the women: When they saw the resurrected Lord, they grabbed His feet. What do you do when you come before the presence of God and when you come to the church of God? When the people are singing praises to God, what is your reaction? When they saw the Lord, they worshipped Him.

I dare say that some of you are like the next category mentioned in verse seventeen:

but some were doubtful.

Brothers and sisters, we need to cultivate and to develop our worship to God. When we see Him and when we are in His presence, we need to kneel down and bow our hearts to Him.

We have said that witnessing is telling others what you have seen, what you have heard and what you have experienced. If you do not keep your appointments with the Lord and if you do not learn how to worship Him, you will have nothing to witness because you have not seen anything, you have not heard anything and you have not experienced anything. That is why you have nothing to say. There is no joy and no peace coming out from your heart. There is no overflow of thanksgiving and gratitude to God. You have nothing to witness. Witnessing is not just sharing the "Four Spiritual Laws" with somebody. It is not sharing a bunch of words to somebody. It is sharing your life and experience.

You know that what you witness is true, because it is true in your heart. You used to witness when you were young. Then you got educated and you started working. You started making money, and then you were bribed. You do not like to have trouble. You are conformed to the world and you have lost sight of the purpose of God, which you used to have. God, help us get rid of this sophisticated attitude and get back to the basics of Your purpose: To make disciples for Your Kingdom. Let us worship the Lord.

Execute the authority from God The Lord said in Mt. 28:18-19:

> All authority has been given to Me in heaven and on earth.
> Go therefore and make disciples . . . .

What kind of authority is it? It is "all authority" which is greater than heaven and earth. Maybe you have seen an angel. Maybe, you have had some spiritual experience, or a dream, or you have seen something in the heavens. That is fine. Put them aside. Look at the authority of the Lord. His authority is greater than heaven and earth, and greater than any king, any government and any boss at your job. Christians are authorized by the Lord to preach. Therefore, make disciples. That is our priority.

You are authorized to be a Sunday School teacher, to be a counselor, and to share the gospel with your friends and your neighbors. You are authorized by the authority of God. Do not let anybody tell you that you cannot do so, because you have been authorized by the King of kings and Lord of lords. Do not lose this opportunity and purpose. The Lord wants us to be His witnesses. Go therefore and make. . ."money?"— not money, but disciples.

Make disciples for God Whenever you serve the Lord, you better ask yourself this question, "Why am I doing this?" And your answer should be "because I want to make disciples." Why are you teaching? It is not just to dispense information, but you want to shape and mold those children that they may become disciples of the Lord. Why are you a counselor or an officer of a fellowship group? You are so that the people you work with may become true followers of Jesus. Why do I preach? I preach to make you become His disciples. Whatever we do, we have to keep this purpose in our mind.

a. Going The Bible says that we are to go. That means as we are going to stores or to restaurants or wherever we are going, we should make disciples for the Lord.

b. Baptizing What follows in verse nineteen is about baptizing. Let us not boast about how many Christians we have won to Christ, but let us boast about how many people we have baptized. If you have led someone to Christ, your job is not finished until that person gets baptized. "Get baptized" means he is committed, he identifies himself with Jesus Christ and His death, and he is not ashamed to be a Christian. He gets baptized to show the world that he is committed to the Church of God. Your job is not finished until that person is baptized. Maybe you are not baptized yet; you need to make sure of your salvation and you need to get baptized. Maybe not in this church, but you must be baptized in a Bible-believing church. Otherwise you will never be a disciple.

c. Teaching It says in verse nineteen that our commission is "going, baptizing and teaching." We do not just teach the commandments and we do not just dispense information, but we teach them to observe the commandments. Brothers and sisters, get away from just giving out information—that is not making disciples. We should teach them to observe the commandments.

We have to get outside the classroom. Teachers, you need to take your students out, and show them how to love as a Christian. When you teach your students a lesson on how to pray, you need to bring them to prayer meeting and show them how it is done. When you teach them devotions, you have to show them how to do it and make sure that it is happening in your lives. Your students ought to see you outside the church building. When we see Christians in their homes, then we know what kind of Christians they truly are. It is not the kind of Christian they are in the church. That counts as well, of course. But it is the kind of Christian they are out in the world. That is the real test and that is what the Lord would judge. Let us get rid of hypocrisy and replace it with true discipleship.

You are not alone in making disciples, because the Lord is with you and His power is there. Brothers and sisters, look for opportunities and be mindful of the purpose of God. Whatever you claim you are doing for the Lord, you should ask yourself, "Why am I doing this? Is it for the purpose of making disciples?" When you talk about Jesus to somebody, when you teach a class, when you are a counselor or an officer, and whatever you are doing, is it for making disciples?

Are we losing sight of the purpose of God, because we have been bribed and because we want to have security? Are we conforming to the world to avoid trouble? God, help us to break out from that mold. Let us get on for the work of God, let us live a simpler life style and let us look for opportunities to make disciples. If you are willing, God will give you opportunities. Oh God, help us see the opportunities. Help us not lose sight and let us see clearly the purpose of God for ourselves, as well as for our church.

WANTED: SONS OF ENCOURAGEMENT

About two weeks ago, I preached on "Coming Out of Depression," and I wanted to emphasize that God's grace was available for that. Not only do we come out of depression on our own effort, but also God has provided other people to help us and God is calling us to help others. We know that, spiritually speaking, we do have a helper. The Holy Spirit is called "the Helper" or "the Comforter" which in Greek is <u>paraklēsis</u> παράκλησις (comforter). This word παράκλησις also describes Jesus Christ when He is called an "Advocate," the one who helps us when we have problems. The Old Testament prophesies that Jesus Christ will be called "Wonderful Counselor." So, God Himself is our helper. He is going to help us and to encourage us. We are sons of God, and we are also called to be "Sons of Encouragement."

Turn with me to Acts 4: 36. Here we see Barnabas. It says in verse thirty-six that his name was Joseph, but he was called "Barnabas" by the apostles. And then the author of Acts, Dr. Luke, gives the translation which means "Son of

Encouragement." How wonderful it is to know the meaning of Barnabas' name. But, it is interesting here—"Barnabas" does not mean "Son of Encouragement." "Barnabas" comes from Hebrew: "Bar" means "son" and "nabas" means "prophecy." He is a "Son of Prophecy," one who speaks for the Lord. This is so wonderful because Luke, under the inspiration of the Holy Spirit, gives us a more interpretative meaning of the name, and it ties in so beautifully with what Dr. Timothy Lin taught us in a seminar, showing us how we ought not only to be teachers but also to be preachers.

What does a prophet of the 20th century do? He speaks for God. It means not only standing behind the pulpit preaching the Bible but also sharing his everyday experiences when he meets with his friends. A prophet needs to give encouragement as well. One who prophesies is one who exalts, encourages and counsels. That is a more progressive revelation of "Barnabas." God has called everyone of us to be a "Son of Encouragement."

The Necessity of Sons of Encouragement

External threats How significant was the presence of Barnabas at this time of Church history? We know from Acts chapter two that when the Holy Spirit came, a great revival occurred. Three thousand people came to know the Lord in one day. Then in Acts chapter three, there was a miracle healing, a great manifestation of God's power. Then we come to Acts chapter four, the persecution. Because the Jewish people did not like what was happening, there was a great persecution against Christians. Great discouragement could have come. But how wonderful that Barnabas, a Son of Encouragement, came at this time when there were needs within the Church. Verse thirty-four talks about how the needs of the people were met.

Brothers and sisters, there are external threats on our church. There are people who do not like our church and do not like us Christians. Anyone who is going to really be a Christian is going to be hated, because the world hates Christ. If you are a member of Christ's body, people will hate you too. You and I are so unaware of what has been happening in each other's life. You are sitting next to someone right now, but you do not know what happened in his life this past week. You do not know his family pressures, his financial pressures, or the difficulties he has gone through.

Internal needs   There are internal pressures as well. There are things happening inside this church you and I are not aware of. The reason why some of you are not aware of these things is because you do not come to prayer meeting. There are real specific needs shared in prayer meeting you do not hear about on Sunday morning. If you just come on Sunday mornings, you will not know the needs of the church, and therefore you cannot be a Son of Encouragement. I can tell you right now God is calling us out to be Sons of Encouragement. The church needs you. Will you not come and be a Son of Encouragement?

There are so many who are discouraged. If you would come to prayer meeting, your heart would ache when you hear some of the needs. That is what it is all about to be a Christian, isn't it? God has called us to a needy world. Do not lock yourself up in your own little world. Extend yourself, come on out to prayer meeting, begin to know the needs of others and pray together for them. Then, you will develop and become a Son of Encouragement.

The Quality of Sons of Encouragement

Barnabas came at the right time. Look at Barnabas' life. It says in verse thirty-six that he "was also called Barnabas by the apostles." Is it not something that the apostles gave him this name? Evidently Barnabas made a great impression upon the apostles; there must have been something wonderful about his life that the disciples would name him "Barnabas." It is like some of us. We give each other different names that we call "nicknames." Why do we call somebody "Lefty"? It is because he is left-handed. Why do we call somebody "Slim" or "Skinny"? It is because he is slim or skinny. Why do we call somebody "Fatso"? It is because we know that he is fat, right? People have different nicknames. I will not tell you my nickname. Barnabas' name was Joseph, but they gave him the nickname "Barnabas," because he made such an impression upon the leaders of the Church.

Properly related to the Church What did Barnabas do? It says in Acts 4:37 that he

> owned a tract of land, sold it and brought the money and
> laid it at the apostles' feet.

Is it not wonderful that he gave money to the church? He gave a great offering. Is that why he was so great? No! Look back at verses thirty-four and thirty-five, and you see that everyone else was doing the same thing. So I scratched my head and said, "What was so special about Barnabas? He was just doing what everybody else was doing, nothing extraordinary." But then the Lord spoke to my heart. That is the key—if you are going to be really a Son of Encouragement, you need to be in co-operation with the church.

a. A total togetherness You cannot do anything separately on your own. Someone may say, "I have a vision from God. What should I do?" Then, he goes off and tries to start his own program, regardless of what the church is doing. He exhausts his own individual effort, so that he can be the leader. That is exactly what God calls us not to do. We are one body, together as one Church. So, do not go off and try to start something on your own. Everything must be brought together as a Church. Yes, we are individuals, but in the Church of God we are one. You think that God has given you a certain vision. Well, that is good. Come to share it with us. Let the pastors and the deacons know. We can let the whole church know, we can pray about it in prayer meeting, and then we can seek the Lord's leading together as a church.

b. **A complete perspective** Many of you are involved in your own fellowship groups. Yes, you are concerned about your particular groups, but not at the expense of leaving out the whole church! You are in a Chinese-speaking fellowship, yet you need to know what is happening in the English-speaking groups. You need to know what is happening in Sunday School. You need to be at prayer meeting. And you need to have a total perspective of what is happening in the church. Barnabas did not do anything special outside of the church. He did what everyone else was doing and he gained the respect of the apostles.

c. **A respectable person** In Acts chapter eleven, we see a new church in the process of forming. The first church was founded in Jerusalem and now a second church was beginning. This was a different thing. You remember in Acts chapter eight, the Samaritans were receiving the Lord, and many of them were getting excited up north in Samaria. What did the church in Jerusalem do? They sent some representatives to see what was happening there. Whom did they send? They sent Peter and John to make sure that there was still a connection with the mother church, because nothing individual was to happen. Peter and John were the apostles of the church.

And now, here in Acts chapter eleven, another such incident was happening. There were people being won to Christ, even gentiles, in Antioch. The mother church did not want any individual thing to happen, so they sent a representative again. And whom did they send this time? Verse twenty-two says that they sent Barnabas. But Barnabas was not an apostle. Who was Barnabas? He did not do anything special or anything extraordinary, but evidently he gained the respect of the church. He was trustworthy enough that they sent him. Their sending him shows that he was working in conjunction and in co-operation with the Church of God.

d. A committed member If you are going to be a Son of Encouragement, you need to be properly related to the whole church. Are you a member of this church? May God help you to see that you need to be a member of a church. Maybe you have been coming here for years and years. If God has called you to be here, why do you not join and be properly related to the Church of God? And if this is not your church, then go find a church. As a church, we are not crying out for new members, but we are more than welcome to receive those who have been called by God. You ought to join one church. It does not have to be this one, but you ought to join one church, or you can never be a Son of Encouragement.

e. A God-first Christian What did Barnabas do as a Son of Encouragement? Acts 11:23 says:

he had come and witnessed the grace of God . . . .

A Son of Encouragement can see the grace of God. This was a brand new work in Antioch, and Barnabas saw the grace of

God. When a new work begins, you and I approach it with suspicion and caution. But, Barnabas could see the grace of God evident. The next thing he did was "he rejoiced." When you see a new work, do you rejoice? Again, you and I may question and say, "We don't know what's happening there." But then, Barnabas

> began to encourage them all with resolute heart to remain true to the Lord . . . . (Acts 11:23)

A Son of Encouragement will encourage people to remain true to the Lord. He will encourage them to be dedicated to God's truth and bear fruit. As a result, "considerable numbers were brought to the Lord" (Acts 11:24). And verse twenty-five is wonderful—"And he left . . . ." Barnabas left for Tarsus to look for Saul. A Son of Encouragement does not look for glory for himself, but always looks for people to help him. He does not claim, "This is mine," but he recruits help from other people. So Barnabas found Saul in Tarsus, and they stayed in Antioch for a year.

Brothers and sisters, God has called us to be Sons of Encouragement. We need to be properly related to a church and to see with the perspective of the whole church. Thus, when we see new works happen, we will see the grace of God: how God uses different groups and different works, and how He brings them together for the full purpose of His Church! And God has called you and me to see that.

Fully empowered by the Lord

a. Full of goodness There is another requirement— you need to be fully empowered by the Lord. Acts 11:24 says:

> he was a good man . . . .

A Son of Encouragement must be a good man. You have to be a good Christian; you have to be a Christian with good moral conduct. When people see you as good and trustworthy, they will trust you. Do you remember the little boy who talked to this elderly lady? The little boy was standing by the lake and he asked this lady, "Lady, are you a Christian?" And the lady said, "Well, I read my Bible." The little boy said, "But, I mean, are you a Christian?" And the lady said, "Well, I pray." "But are you really a Christian?" "Well, I go to church." The little boy said, "Please, lady, are you a Christian?" And finally the lady gave the right answer and said, "I have accepted Christ into my heart." Then the little boy said, "Oh, I'm so glad that you are a Christian. I have a quarter. Will you hold my quarter so that I can go swimming?" The world is looking for good people. Christians ought to be good people. If you are not a good person, you cannot be a Son of Encouragement.

b. Full of the Holy Spirit Barnabas was full of the Holy Spirit. He did not have to pray, "Lord, fill me with the Holy Spirit," because he was already full of the Holy Spirit. You and I need to be constantly filled with the Holy Spirit. We ought to yield to God, be sensitive to his leading and pray without ceasing.

c. Full of faith Not only was Barnabas full of the Holy Spirit, he was also full of faith. He believed in God fully. Faith comes by hearing and hearing by the Word of God. Do not be so smart, because the only way you are going to have faith is by reading God's Word. Some think that they know everything without reading God's Word. There is no short cut. If you want to have a good faith and be full of faith, you need to read God's Word. You need to read God's Word and apply God's Word. Get into God's Word!

There was an intellectual college professor sitting in a boat, and an old man was rowing the boat. They were rowing across a big river. As they were going across the river, the college professor asked the boatman and said, "Do you know anything about philosophy?" The old man rowing the boat said, "No, I've never heard of the word." The professor said, "Well, I'm sorry. One-fourth of your life is gone." Then, the professor asked the boatman, "Do you know anything about astronomy or physics?" The old boatman said, "I don't know anything about astronomy or physics." The prideful professor said, "Well, man, I'm sorry. Three-fourth of your life is gone." Then suddenly a wave hit the boat and it tipped over. They both fell into the water. The old man cried out, "Professor, can you swim?" He said, "No, I can't!" And the boatman said, "Well, then, your whole life is gone!" Do not be so smart. We think we know so much, but you and I have not even scratched the surface of what God has for us. You need to get into God's Word.

There is no substitute for reading God's Word. We not only have to read it but also have to act upon it. God's Word says "to witness," and there is a person sitting next to you, maybe on the bus or maybe on the airplane. You say, "I know God's Word. He says that I should witness to him." Then, act upon it and do it! But you say, "I don't feel like it." "I'm too scared." "I don't know what he'll say to me." "I don't know what I'll say." No, you just do it. Do not go by your feelings. When you do it, God will bless you. When you do it, you are witnessing by faith. You do not know what you are going to say. You do not know how he is going to respond. All you know is a sure word of prophecy. "He says, 'do it,' and I do it." If you do it by faith, you will watch God bless you and watch your faith increase. Read God's Word and act upon it. A Son of Encouragement is full of faith.

The Ministry of Sons of Encouragement

What did Barnabas do? Acts 11:25 says, "he left for Tarsus to look for Saul." Who was Saul of Tarsus? Well, later he had become the great apostle Paul. If you go back to

Acts chapter nine, you will see that Saul was a Pharisee and a murderer. He was the head of a group persecuting Christians. In Acts chapter nine, he came to know Jesus Christ. Think of a person that is most impossible to ever become a Christian. Maybe you will say, "My father, he'll never become a Christian," or there is a friend you know and you will say "never, never, never." Brothers and sisters, it is possible. Paul was an impossible case, yet he came to know the Lord. In Acts chapter nine, we see him come to know the Lord on the road to Damascus.

After Paul came to know the Lord, he went to Jerusalem trying to get to know the disciples (Acts 9:26), but they were afraid of him. They did not believe that he had become a disciple. So what was Saul to do? There he was again— Barnabas, the Son of Encouragement, was the one who took Saul in and introduced him to the rest of the apostles. Barnabas could see again the grace of God, and he saw the potential in this young man Saul. No one would take him, but Barnabas did. He was the one who could see the potential in people.

Recognizing potential Who is to tell what God can do for your life? D. L. Moody was a great evangelist, but he used to be a shoe salesman. He had a Son of Encouragement, Edward Kimball. You will say, "Who has heard of Kimball?" But he is famous now because he was the Son of Encouragement that brought up D. L. Moody. There was another great evangelist in the early 1900's named Billy Sunday, and what a great evangelist he was. He used to be a baseball player. His Son of Encouragement was Harry Monroe. "Who has heard of Monroe?" Ah, but, he is famous; he is famous in God's eyes, because he was Billy Sunday's Son of Encouragement. Everybody knows Billy Graham, but no one knows Mordecai Ham. Who is Mordecai Ham? He was Billy Graham's Son of Encouragement. The Father of Missions is William Carey, and everybody knows William Carey. But who has heard of William Ward? Or Dr. John Thomas? Or Mr. Chater? Yet, these were William Carey's Sons of Encouragement. Everybody has heard of Charles Finney, the great revivalist of continents all over the world, but no one has heard of the young prayer warriors that helped Finney along his ministry. Maybe no one will ever hear of you as a Son of Encouragement, but maybe God will give you the grace to see the potential in other souls and become a Son of Encouragement. As for these people whom you are helping, who knows what God will do with them?

Remaining persistent Barnabas not only saw the potential in Saul but also saw the potential in another young man. Turn with me to Acts chapter fifteen. We know that Barnabas and Paul went out on the first missionary journey and started many churches. Then when we come to Acts 15:36, the second journey begins. Paul said to Barnabas, "Let us return and visit the brethren." Verse thirty-seven says that:

> Barnabas was desirous of taking John, called Mark, along with them also.

We know that when Peter was in prison, many Christians had an all-night prayer meeting at the home of Mark's mother (Acts 12:12). We also know that Mark went with Paul and Barnabas on the first missionary journey, but later, deserted them (Acts 13:13). He could not take it; he went home. So it says here in Acts 15:38 that Paul kept insisting not to take Mark along because Mark deserted them. But Barnabas wanted to take Mark and, of course, Mark was his cousin.

Barnabas maintained that there was potential in this young man Mark. "Yes, he made a mistake, but I believe in him. Let's bring him along." Paul said," No!" And the disagreement was so sharp that they parted. Even Barnabas

203

left Paul. It says that Barnabas took Mark with him to Cyprus.
That is the last that we hear of Barnabas in the book of Acts.
And of course, Paul rose up to great prominence.

Does that mean Barnabas was wrong? Was he a stubborn
old fool? He should have stuck with Paul and left Mark at
home. But Barnabas was persistent. He saw the potential in
Mark, and he knew that Mark would become a great leader.
Can you imagine what Mark was feeling? "There is the great
missionary Barnabas, and there is the great apostle Paul. They
are fighting like cats and dogs. And why are they fighting? It
is because of me! It is my fault! They are arguing over me.
This great team will split because of me!"

What happened to Barnabas? What happened to Mark?
We see later in the Corinthian epistles that Paul spoke dearly of
Barnabas. Turn with me to Colossians 4:10. At this time Paul
was in prison. He was sending greetings from Aristarchus to
the Colossian Christians, and there he mentioned Barnabas'
cousin Mark:

> (about whom you received instructions: if he comes to
> you, welcome him)

It is possible that Barnabas had gone home to be with the Lord
by then, but Mark came back in favor with Paul. The last
epistle from Paul was 2 Timothy, for soon after 2 Timothy was
written, Paul was beheaded. Here at the end of Paul's life in 2
Timothy 4:11 Paul said:

> Only Luke is with me. Pick up Mark and bring him with
> you, for he is useful to me for service.

Now, we see that it is Mark who became useful to Paul.
Barnabas was the one who encouraged Paul and encouraged
Mark. They both became the great men that they were and, of
course, Mark became the one who wrote the Gospel according
to Mark.

I believe that Paul learned from Barnabas, because Paul himself became a Son of Encouragement. There was a slave who stole money from his master. The slave was Onesimus and the master, Philemon. Paul took Onesimus in and led him to Christ, and wrote a letter to Philemon encouraging him to receive back Onesimus. Paul's epistles to Timothy and Titus are letters of encouragement also.

Brothers and sisters, God calls you and me to be Sons of Encouragement. But first of all you need to be properly related to the Church of God, and you need to be fully empowered by the Lord. When these happen, you will be able to see the grace of God, the needs of others and the potential in people. As you work with them, you will find out that God will use them. You should be persistent in that. Will you give yourselves to be Sons of Encouragement? God's Church needs you; we need more Barnabases.

A MISSIONS-MINDED CHURCH

The Purpose for Its Existence

Let us turn to John chapter seventeen. I want you to note two things in this prayer concerning missions. In verse fifteen, Jesus says:

> I do not ask Thee to take them out of the world, but to keep them from the evil one.

Evil is not just some force in the world. There is a personality to evil and that is the Devil. Here, Jesus prays for our protection from the Devil, but not for us to be taken away from the world. This world belongs to the Devil at this moment, and so do all its values and systems. The Lord has called us to take this world and win people to Jesus Christ. Every time when we do that, we are taking ground away from the Devil and trespassing on forbidden territory. The Devil does not like it, so he will form his strategy to stop us.

Diabolic Manipulation The Lord says in verse fourteen that because we have been given the Word, the world has hated us. Why? It is because we are not of this world, even as the Lord is not of this world. Nobody likes to be hated. It does not feel good psychologically. We do not want the world to hate us. So what do we do? We begin to compromise or conform ourselves to the world and thus fall into the diabolical manipulations.

a. The world hates us The Lord has told us that the world will hate us. If there is not any hatred toward us in any form, any way or any measure, something might be wrong. I am not saying that we are to go around trying to make the world hate us. But if we are just faithful to His Word, the natural outcome will be that the world will hate us. To live as strangers and sojourners in this world, we will find that the world will hate us. They will not agree to our methods, they will not like our philosophies and they will say, "Why are you so fanatical?" That is the kind of hatred that will come.

b. The Devil stops us Knowing of Satan's diabolical schemes should make us all the more missions-minded. We know what Satan is trying to do, so we are determined more than ever to be missions-minded. This is the negative aspect of why we must be missions-minded. Because the Devil will try every means to stop us, we will find ourselves easily entrapped into worldly schemes: More interested in riches than in souls; more concerned about our own comforts than reaching out to others. We do not care about the rest of the world but ourselves. That is Satan's trick! Therefore, we must determine that we will be missions-minded.

c. The battle needs us We are to be in the forefront of the battle. Who here has a young heart with the adventurous spirit to fight the battle, to carry the banner of Jesus Christ, and never let it fall? Who here wants to be in the front line of the battle? That is where the Lord calls us to be; and we can be sure that Satan is on the opposing front line. We have the promise of victory, but it is not going to happen unless we apply it. Therefore, we need to be that church which the Lord is building, that church which will go forward and that church which the gates of Hades will not prevail against. But, we have become a church that falls into the world's trap. We care about our own riches; we do not push out to win souls for Christ. May God help us to be missions-minded.

Divine Mandate There is a positive reason to be missions-minded: We have a divine mandate. The Lord Himself has called us to it. In John 17:18 His prayer is:

> As Thou didst send Me into the world, I also have sent them into the world.

Elsewhere in John 20:21 He says:

> as the Father has sent Me, I also send you.

a. Jesus' missionary methods Jesus was sent by the Father, and we are sent by Jesus. In what manner was Jesus sent? It might be good for us to look at, shall we say, the "missionary methods" of Jesus Christ. When Jesus came, He identified with people. He came and took upon Himself the form of a man and of a servant. He came to serve us. To find Man, He became a man; to win the Jews, He became a Jew. We will never find Him identifying Himself with any "class" of people. He talked to the rich as well as the poor. He identified with people.

We see that Jesus went out to find people. He did not come to build a temple and call people to the temple. But, instead He went to the streets; He went to the cities; He went to their homes; and He went to their villages to find them. We find Jesus on the hillside, at the seashore, at a banquet and by a well. Jesus went out to find people.

We see that Jesus chose men to do His work. He trained

men for three years and then He Himself left the field. He wanted the congregation to be self-supporting, self-propagating, and self-sufficient. He wanted all to be under the guidance of the Holy Spirit. Jesus was financed by faith. He preached the gospel without charge. Judas kept the purse for all the disciples and it met their simplest needs. Jesus never worried about money.

Jesus obeyed the law of the government, paid tribute to Caesar and submitted Himself to the trial of Pontius Pilate. He did not try to reform the religion of His day. He did not try to change the government. He did not try to twist society. He did not change slavery, but spoke to the slaves. He just preached the gospel, and let its own dynamic power change lives. We see that Jesus never compromised—He faced opposition, He faced danger, He faced criticism, He faced success, and He faced failure. And, He never wavered from His purpose. He had absolute conformity to the will and the Word of God. These are some of the "missionary methods" of our Lord Jesus Christ.

b. Antioch's missions-minded model As He has been sent, so He sends you and me. We have a divine mandate from God to do missions, and thus as a church, we need to be missions-minded. We have a wonderful example of the missions-minded church at Antioch. What is so special about the church at Antioch? It is just like any other congregation. In fact, Acts 9:31 tells us that there was one church throughout all Judea, Galilee and Samaria. There must have been many congregations in all those regions, yet they called themselves one church. This is not unlike the idea of our branch churches. Although we have our branch churches, yet we are one Church.

So what is so special about the church at Antioch? Acts 11:19 says that because of persecution many Christians from the Jerusalem church went out to different lands and that they spoke the Word to no one except the Jews. However, in verse twenty, we see a contrast:

> But there were some of them, men of Cyprus and Cyrene, who came to Antioch and began speaking to the Greeks also . . . .

That is what is so special about this church—it was the first church that had a combination of Jews and Greeks (gentiles) in one church. It was very unusual in those days. It was a church without prejudice; a church that broke down the wall of partition between Jews and gentiles.

Besides this, the church at Antioch was not established by the apostles or any representative from Jerusalem, but by men of Cyprus and Cyrene, whose names we do not know. They are unknown to us, but they are known to God. Many missionaries, whom we do not know, are planting churches all over the world. We do not know their names, but God knows them. You can be sure of that. Maybe one here among us will be a missionary. Not too many people will know your name and the world will hate you, but God knows your name. Be faithful to Him.

The Preparation for Its Establishment

The Scripture begins to reveal to us what a church ought to have, and when a church has these things, it will be missions-minded.

Receptivity Verse 22 says that after the church at Antioch began to grow, it began to grow and grow and grow, and the news reached Jerusalem. As soon as the news reached the ears of the church at Jerusalem, they sent Barnabas off to Antioch. Antioch is far north of Jerusalem, in the land of Syria. They sent Barnabas to check it out. That was, in a sense, common for all these churches. When a church started in Samaria, the church at Jerusalem sent Peter and John to check it out. But, there is something unusual here, because Barnabas was not an apostle.

a. To Barnabas Who in the world is Barnabas? Well, let us go back to Acts 4:36. There was a man named Joseph, and he was called Barnabas. Barnabas was not his real name. He was Joseph but he was given the nickname, Barnabas. Barnabas means "Son of Encouragement." Barnabas was one who could refresh the souls. He knew how to build up people and how to say positive things to people. The word "encouragement" is the same word that describes the Holy Spirit as the Comforter (Jn. 14:16) and Jesus Christ as our Advocate. Barnabas was a Son of Encouragement. Who gave Barnabas the nickname? He was called Barnabas by the apostles! So, he made a distinct impression upon the apostles.

We see that in Acts 4:37, he owned a tract of land, but he sold it and gave the money to the Lord through the apostles. He was a well respected person, a generous man and a man who loved the Lord and the Church. That qualified Barnabas to be sent off as a representative to Antioch. Furthermore, Acts 11:24 says that Barnabas "was a good man, and full of the Holy Spirit and of faith." So Barnabas had such spiritual qualities as well.

Something we might notice about the church at Antioch: They were readily receptive to the coming of Barnabas. They did not say, "Who are you? What are you doing here? This is our church! Why don't you go back to Jerusalem?" No, they received Barnabas and let Barnabas teach them, because they recognized that Barnabas was full of the Holy Spirit and of faith.

b. To Saul Now what did Barnabas do? Barnabas brought a lot of people to the Lord. There were so many people that he could not handle them all by himself. Therefore, Acts 11:25 says, "he left for Tarsus to look for Saul." Tarsus is even further north. Barnabas went there to look for Saul. Who was Saul? Saul was a Pharisee dramatically converted to Christianity on the road to Damascus. He persecuted Christians before. When he became a Christian, he tried to go to the apostles, but the apostles were very hesitant to accept him. "Oh, no, stay away from us!" It was not until Barnabas took Saul to the apostles, that the apostles received him. After a while, Saul's preaching caused a lot of disturbance among the Jews, and the apostles thought, "Oh, too much trouble!" So, they sent Saul back up to Tarsus, his home town. Saul had to wait and wait and wait. He could not do anything for the Lord, until Barnabas brought him down to Antioch.

What did the church at Antioch do? Again, unlike the apostles who were a little bit wary about Saul, they opened their door and welcomed him. A church that is getting ready to be missions-minded is one that readily receives people. In fact, they let Barnabas and Saul stay there for over a year to teach them. This church could recognize a good person, a person full of the Holy Spirit and of faith.

I wonder if our church can do that. Are we ready to receive prophets and teachers who teach the Word of God? I hope so. Oh, I wish we can recognize such people. When missionaries come to our church, we would readily receive them, go out of our way to meet them, shake their hands and get to know them. Get to know some of our guest speakers. As a church, we learn together to be receptive to those people who love the Lord. Then, we are on the way to be missions-minded. If we cannot learn to love and receive our own people, how can we learn to receive people who are without Christ?

c. To Agabus Acts 11:27 says that more prophets

came from Jerusalem, especially one named Agabus. We may ask, "Who in the world is Agabus?" Probably, the Christians in Antioch might have said the same thing, "Who is Agabus?" But again, the church at Antioch readily received these prophets.

Sensitivity In verse twenty-eight, the Bible says that Agabus stood up and began to indicate, by the Spirit of God, that there would be a famine in Jerusalem. What did the Antioch church do? They said, "Let's get together. We're determined. We're going to make a contribution to help the famine relief." This is amazing! The church heard the message—a prophecy that there is going to be a famine in Jerusalem—and the church said, "Okay, we're going to take an offering. Dig into your pockets, get the money and we're determined to help the famine relief." But, the famine had not happened yet! They just got a word from Agabus! Do we see how sensitive the church was to the Holy Spirit? They easily recognized that, ". . .yes, this is Agabus, but the Spirit of God is speaking!" They responded to the needs even before the event occurred. That is unusual sensitivity.

Generosity Some might say, "Helping famine relief is not missions. They are just helping their fellow brothers and sisters in Jerusalem." Maybe that is not missions as far as leading people to Christ, but that is the beginning of being missions-minded. A lot of people at Antioch did not even know who these Christians in Jerusalem were, because transportation was not good. They had no telephones and no televisions; it was not easy to travel between Jerusalem and Antioch. So a lot of them did not know who these Christians were. But, they got this message and they sent the relief.

Our church has an opportunity to help famine relief in Ethiopia. We do not even know who these Christians in Ethiopia are, and a lot of them are not Christians. We have an opportunity. I hope that we will pray about it, and we will see if the Lord makes us missions-minded.

The church at Antioch was not only receptive but also sensitive to the Spirit of God and generous to others. May God help us to be generous with our money to help those who have needs. We have many opportunities for that. God will bless our church if we do so. Let us be generous. Give liberally. That will make us missions-minded. It will take away the thoughts of worldly riches Satan is trying to implant in us. To be generous will free us to be missions-minded. As long as we hoard up our riches, we will never be missions-minded, and Satan has got us in his hands. Be determined as these Christians were—determined to send a contribution. May God help us be determined individuals, that we may in turn be a determined church.

Principles for Its Execution

I believe that we are receptive to God's teachers; we are somewhat sensitive to the leading of the Holy Spirit; and as a church, we are very generous. Of course, we need to improve. I really feel that our church is at the threshold of being truly missions-minded. We must press on further. The church at Antioch went further.

Obeying the Holy Spirit's call
a. Operating according to spiritual gifts We remember that in Acts chapter eleven, there were many people being won to Christ, so there must have been a lot of people in the church. Here in Acts 13:1, they were focusing on their prophets and teachers. Do you know what this tells us? A church that is going to be missions-minded is operating according to spiritual gifts.

That is what we need in our church. It is of no use to

force people to be in a certain position in the church, when their spiritual gifts are not aligned with that position. Our leadership in this church is committed to help each Christian to find his/her spiritual gifts, and then to find avenues of service where each fits. I believe that if we operate according to spiritual gifts, oh, the Holy Spirit is really going to speak to us. Everybody needs to know the responsibilities of his/her own spiritual gifts. Let us function that way, and I believe that the Holy Spirit will really speak to us.

Let us meet the prophets and teachers in this church at Antioch. Besides Saul, there were Barnabas, whom we have already met, and Simeon, who was called "Niger." Niger means black, so probably he was a black African. But, there he was in the church at Antioch as one of their teachers. Then, we see Lucius of Cyrene. Lucius is a Roman name, so he was probably a Roman gentile. And we see Manaen who had been brought up with Herod the tetrarch. That means Manaen was a foster brother of Herod the tetrarch.

Who was Herod the tetrarch? He was the wicked one who cut off the head of John the Baptist. Manaen and Herod grew up together, but Manaen found Christ, and thus their paths separated. How true that has been with some of us here! We grew up with certain friends, but when we found Christ and they have not, our paths separated.

With such diverse backgrounds, yet they all were prophets and teachers of the same church. We have many people here today in our church with diverse backgrounds: Some are from Hong Kong; some, from Taiwan; and some, from Malaysia. We have some who are not Chinese, and some who are first, second or third generation American-born Chinese. We all come from different backgrounds and with different educations. But, we all have spiritual gifts. We are not united by economic class or social class, but by the sovereign power of the Holy Spirit. Find your spiritual gift, so we can function together. We can have a computer expert, a janitor or a president of a bank, but we can all be prophets and teachers of the church. It depends on the Spirit of God. Oh, let the church operate according to spiritual gifts!

b. ***Worshipping God in public continuously***
Acts 13:2 says that they were ministering to the Lord. This word, "ministering to the Lord" is where we get the word "liturgy" which means "public worship." This verb is in the present tense, which means that they were worshipping and worshipping and worshipping all the time. The church that is going to be missions-minded needs to be in continuous worship. This is public worship—to be unafraid of the public; to worship out in the open. That is when the Holy Spirit will speak. We need to be the ones who are worshipping at all times.

You may say, "I come to worship service every week." That is good. However, your body may be here, yet your heart may not. Make sure you lift up the name of the Lord and worship Him with all your heart. If someone is absent from worship, we will call him up, because we are concerned about his worship. This is a priority of our church. That is why we have everyone fill out a registration slip. If you miss one time, we will call you because we care: Maybe you have been sick; maybe you are backsliding. We will call you. We will try our best. Sometimes we may miss, but we will try our best. So, worship the Lord continuously, and the Spirit of God will speak to us.

c. ***Fasting and praying unceasingly*** In addition, it says in Acts 13:2 that they were fasting. Fasting goes along with serious prayer. The verb is in the present tense, so they were fasting and fasting and fasting and fasting! They were serious with God and they were serious in prayer. It does not mean that they never ate at all, but they had continuous times of fasting and prayer. This is something we need to improve in our church. Usually, we have fasting once a year, but maybe we need to fast more often. That will make us missions-minded. The church at Antioch was engaged in three things:

1. Operating according to spiritual gifts,
2. Publicly worshipping the Lord continuously, and
3. Fasting and praying unceasingly.

Identifying with the work

a. The urgency of time In the midst of these actions, the Holy Spirit spoke. Oh, may He do that in our midst. Right in the middle of their prayer and their worship, they heard the voice of the Holy Spirit. There is a Greek word that has not been translated in the English Bible because it is hard to translate. It is just a tiny little word, but it makes all the difference in the world. When the Holy Spirit said, "Set apart for me Barnabas and Saul," there is a little word that needs to be added. The sense of the word is "right now there is an urgency!" There is an urgency right now today! Even Jesus said so:

> The harvest is plentiful, but the laborers are few . . . . (Lk. 10:2)
> Look on the fields, that they are white for harvest. (Jn. 4:35)

Right now we need somebody! The Holy Spirit is looking for a missions-minded church, out of which there can be some Barnabases and Sauls. There is a desperate urgency in this verse.

b. The calling of God How did the Holy Spirit speak? It could be that the whole congregation heard it, or maybe only the prophets and teachers heard it, or it could be like the Macedonian call in Acts chapter sixteen, where only Saul heard it. When they shared it with the church, the church prayed and confirmed the calling. By God's grace, the same may happen in our midst. Maybe somebody here has really sensed in his heart that the Holy Spirit is calling him for missions. Then, by all means, share it with our pastors and our deacons. We will pray with you and we will sense together the confirmation from the Holy Spirit. By God's grace, you will go.

c. The laying of hands It says here in the Bible that after they heard the call of the Holy Spirit, they prayed and fasted, and then laid hands on them and sent them away. "To lay hands" means you identify with the work. We do not just send a missionary out and then wipe our hands and say, "That's it." No, when our elders lay hands, that means we identify with the missionary—when he goes out, we are going with him. We need to be informed of what is happening in the field, so that we can identify with their work and know how to pray for them. When we hear of their financial need, we might give to their need. They are still one with us, even though they might be in a distant land, because we identify with their work by the laying of hands. So, we do not just send them out and leave them alone.

Releasing the gifted personnel Now take notice of something interesting in Acts 13:3-4. Verse three says, "they sent them away," but verse four says, "So, being sent out by the Holy Spirit"! Who sends, the church or the Holy Spirit? Well, they are two different words in Greek. The word "send" in verse three means "to release" and "to let loose," while that in verse four is "to send." Therefore, it is the Holy Spirit who sends. As a missions-minded church, who are we to stop the ministry of the Holy Spirit? The Holy Spirit is calling certain people and we, as a church, sense it, confirm it, lay our hands on them and release them. That is what the Church does. We do not send people; the Holy Spirit does. We identify with them and release them to the grace of God. May God really speak to our hearts today that we will really understand about missions and be this kind of Church.

How wonderful that as a church we have released Dr. Lin, so that he can be free to minister in Taiwan. We have released other members of our pastoral staff to speak in other places: Dr. Murphy Lum at our Westminster Branch, Dr. Jackson Lau at our San Gabriel Branch, and some members to lead workshops at the West Coast Chinese Christian Conference. We identify with them and work with them in prayer. May the Lord lead us, so that we can release some for the missions field.

We want to be a missions-minded church. To do that, we need a missions-minded people. Satan is against all missionary endeavors, so we must not let worldly comforts deter us from this goal. Since we have the divine mandate from Jesus Christ Himself, we must be missions-minded. There is no other way. Otherwise, judgment will come upon this church. Let us be receptive to one another, show hospitality and meet the missionaries and guest speakers that come our way. Let us listen to the teaching of God's Word, be receptive and sensitive to the Holy Spirit, and be generous in our giving. Let us find our spiritual gifts and operate accordingly in the church. Let us always be worshipping and praying to the Lord. Let us watch the Holy Spirit speak. Then, we will be on the way, like the church at Antioch, to be a missions-minded Church.

APPENDIX

IN REMEMBRANCE OF
GREGORY ROBERT OWYANG

"For to me, to live is Christ, and to die is gain" (Phil. 1:21) provided "Dr. Greg," as he was affectionately known, a constant source of courage and strength to meet each day. He desired to be remembered as "a man who loved the Lord dearly and faithfully served Him till the end." He is remembered for this and more.

Gregory Robert Owyang, chosen by his senior class as "the most likely to succeed," was born in San Mateo, California, on July 25, 1948. He was the fourth of six sons of Dr. Edwin and Alyce Owyang. As a youth, he excelled in academics, athletics, music and leadership.

In 1963, as a teenager, he accepted Christ. Realizing that "faith, if it has no works, is dead" (Jas. 2:17), Greg dedicated his life to Jesus at a Christian conference in 1968. The direction of his life was changed; his early aspiration to become a doctor turned into a passion for the Lord and His Word. After graduating from the University of California at Davis with a major in zoology in 1970, he entered Talbot Thelogical

Seminary where he received his Master of Divinity degree. He later earned his doctorate in 1974 from Fuller Theological Seminary.

His burden for lost souls, especially among Chinese young people, led him to seek help in learning Cantonese. Annie Poon, a foreign student at Biola College, offered to tutor Greg. Annie later became his lovely wife.

Just as clearly as the Lord had called Dr. Greg to be His servant, it was also His will for him to come to the First Chinese Baptist Church of Los Angeles in 1970. At this thriving church in Chinatown, there were many opportunities for service and training. Dr. Greg's zeal for the Lord, love of sharing Christ through music, and straightforward sincerity readily won the hearts of the people. The discipling relationship and support of the senior pastor, Dr. Timothy Lin, prepared him well to face the many pastoral responsibilities he was later to assume. He was ordained in 1975 and called to be Assistant Pastor in 1978.

Dr. Greg's unique ability to make God's Word understandable and come alive opened up a ministry for him in the Church's various fellowship groups as speaker, workshop leader and Bible teacher. His special gift of preaching was recognized far beyond the confines of the local church. He spoke at revival meetings, evangelistic services, Christian retreats and camps throughout the United States and Canada. As the Lord gave him opportunities to speak, Dr. Greg often specified that his sermons be translated into Chinese. This was one means that enabled him to minister to very diverse audiences. God used him to turn the spiritual tide for whole churches as well as for individuals. Many echoed "Amen," when one sister testified, "I have not been the same since the revival meeting Dr. Greg led in our church. He electrified us. He stirred our hearts. His love for the Lord and people was so evident. We caught his love."

Pastor Owyang was a preacher who stood for the truth and authority of all Scripture. He applied it to all areas of his own life as boldly as he proclaimed it. Gentle in the face of personal criticism, he never backed down an inch where Scripture was concerned. He was not afraid to confront others with truths from God's Word for he knew well the power it had to pierce men's souls. He would often say, "If God says to do it in His Word, then do it! What are you waiting for?"

His fierce love for the Word of God was tenderly expressed in his concern for others. Dr. Greg placed the cares of others above his own. His days were filled with prayer and fasting for those the Lord has entrusted to his care. In addition to discipling, counseling, visiting the sick and being available to support and comfort others, Dr. Greg also had the special ability to bring out the best in people, often resulting in brothers and sisters learning new joy in serving God through his example and positive approach to life.

Dr. Greg's intimate knowledge of the mind and heart of God and his total trust and love of our Lord Jesus Christ allowed him, by God's grace, through the Holy Spirit, to lead and challenge God's people. One of the ways he expressed this best was through music. Whether he was playing the guitar, piano or singing, his joy and enthusiasm were clearly communicated. He is remembered for such songs as "He Is God," "To Be God's People" and "The Greatest Thing in All My Life." God used these and many other songs to stir the hearts of His people to new heights of love and worship.

Described as a "Chinese Billy Graham," Dr. Greg frequently had praises and expressions of gratitude heaped upon him. However, Dr. Greg did not seek the high esteem of others, nor did he dwell on past accomplishments, but sincerely prayed, "Let me not look for man's praises and be proud, but let men see my good works and glorify God."

Greg had great enthusiasm for his role as husband and father. He showered his wife Annie with love and affection. He supported and honored her as a co-heir in God's Kingdom. He was both father and friend to his children, Jason Bryan, Joshua Stephen and Karissa Joy. Ever conscious that a Christ-centered and balanced upbringing was important, he saw to it that their family worship time was both meaningful and enjoyable. Annie described their life together as "heaven on earth."

Just as he had lived for God, Dr. Greg was prepared and willing to die for God. On June 30, 1985, he was fatally wounded on the sanctuary's platform. Although it was untimely in the sight of men, his homegoing has come according to God's will. He is greatly missed, but his vibrant life, characterized by a singleness of purpose in serving the Lord, has left an indelible impression.

"A simple man, a good man and a man of great faith, hope and love"—Gregory Robert Owyang was a man God found worthy to die for His name's sake. We remember him with hearts of thanksgiving to God. Through his life, we have experienced God's goodness and joy.

Born: July 25, 1948
Home going: July 1, 1985

Chronology of the Sermons

Taking A Stand For God	1/22/84
Take Hold Of Eternal Life	10/31/82
How Personal Is Your God?	2/27/83
He Who Is Spiritual - Part I	7/26/81
He Who Is Spiritual - Part II	8/ 2/81
When I Cry, God Is Silent	12/26/82
God's Grace To Do God's Will	9/26/82
Spiritual Warfare	2/ 7/82
What Happens When I Sin?	10/11/81
The Battle Within	5/ 3/81
Lord, Increase Our Faith!	2/22/81
How To Love God	9/12/82
To Be Great In God's Kingdom	1/ 4/81
Let Us Not Lose Sight Of Our Purpose	12/ 5/82
Wanted: Sons Of Encouragement	2/ 1/81
A Missions-Minded Church	11/29/81